COMPREHENSION: GRADE 3
TABLE OF CONTENTS

www.svschoolsupply.com

© Steck-Vaughn Company

Comprehension 3, SV 6185-0

INTRODUCTION

This book is designed to help students become better readers. The IRA/NCTE Standards for the English Language Arts lists as their first recommendation: "Students read a wide range of print and nonprint texts to build an understanding of texts, of themselves, and of the cultures of the United States and the world; to acquire new information; to respond to the needs and demands of society and the workplace; and for personal fulfillment. Among these texts are fiction and nonfiction, classic and contemporary works." A variety of reading selections attract and hold the interest of students. The activities in this book contain high-interest reading selections that cover a wide range of subjects in such areas as science, social studies, history, sports, and the arts.

ORGANIZATION

Each of the six units focuses on essential reading comprehension skills: finding the facts, detecting a sequence, learning new vocabulary through context, identifying the main idea, drawing conclusions, and making inferences.

- **FACTS:** Literal comprehension is a foundation skill for understanding a reading selection. Students using the Facts unit practice identifying pieces of factual information presented in each reading selection. The focus is on specific details that tell who, what, when, where, and how.

- **SEQUENCE:** Sequence involves the time order of events and the temporal relationship of one event or step to other events or steps. Reading for sequence means identifying the order of events in a story or the steps in a process.

- **CONTEXT:** When students practice using context, they must use all the words in a reading selection to understand the unfamiliar words. As they develop this skill, students become aware of the relationships between words, phrases, and sentences. The skill provides them with a tool that helps them understand words and concepts by learning how language is used to express meaning. Mastering this skill allows students to become independent readers.

- **MAIN IDEA:** When students read for the main idea, they must read to recognize the overall point made in the reading selection. Students must be able to differentiate the details from the main idea. They must understand the one idea that is supported by all the details in the selection. Identifying the main idea involves recognizing or making a generalization about a group of specifics.

- **CONCLUSION:** Drawing a conclusion is a complex reading skill because a conclusion is not stated in a reading selection. Students are asked to draw a conclusion based only on the information within a selection. They must put together the details from the information as if they were clues to a puzzle. The conclusion they draw must be supported by the details in the reading selection.

- **INFERENCE:** Students make inferences by combining their own knowledge and experiences with what they read. They must consider all the facts in the reading selection. Then they must put together those facts and what they already know to make a reasonable inference about something that is not stated in the selection. Making an inference requires students to go beyond the information in the text.

USE

The activities in this book are designed for independent use by students who have had instruction in the specific skills covered in the lessons. Copies of the activity sheets can be given to individuals or pairs of students for completion. When students are familiar with the content of the worksheets, they can be assigned as homework.

To begin, determine the implementation that fits your students' needs and your classroom structure. The following plan suggests a format for this implementation.

1. **Administer** the Assessment Test to establish baseline information on each student. This test may also be used as a post-test when the student has completed a unit.

2. **Explain** the purpose of the worksheets to the class.

3. **Review** the mechanics of how you want students to work with the activities. Do you want them to work in pairs? Are the activities for homework?

4. **Introduce** students to the process and purpose of the activities. Work with students when they have difficulty. Give them only a few pages at a time to avoid pressure.

5. **Do** a practice activity together. Review with students how to do each comprehension skill by using the practice example provided in the Overviews.

OVERVIEW: FACTS

Introducing the Skill

Remind students that facts are things they can taste, touch, feel, smell, and see. Explain that successful readers pay close attention to details. Emphasize that the questions in the Facts unit ask about details stated in the reading selections. Students should be able to show where the answer to a question is located in a selection.

How the Lessons Are Organized

A lesson consists of a reading selection about a single topic broken into two parts. Each part is followed by four questions that require students to find the facts in the selection.

Practice Activity

Read this story to your students.

The Earth and the Sun

Long ago a man was thinking about the sky. He had been watching the sun for days. He began to see it in a new way. "The Earth is going around the sun," he said. At that time most people thought the sun went around Earth. They thought Earth was the biggest and best thing in the sky.

The man said, "I must write a book. It might make people angry. But I must tell the truth." The man did write a book. But he never saw it printed. He died in 1543. The book was printed later that year.

People were angry when they read the book. They wanted to think that everything went around Earth. But today people know that the man was right.

Have students answer the following questions about the story.

1. The man had been watching the ___ for days.
   A. moon
   B. Earth
   <u>C. sun</u>

2. The man died in the year ___.
   <u>A. 1543</u>
   B. 1453
   C. 1457

3. The man said, "I must write a ___."
   A. letter
   B. story
   <u>C. book</u>

4. People were ___ when they read the book.
   A. happy
   B. afraid
   <u>C. angry</u>

Explain to students that to find facts, they should read each story very carefully. If they cannot remember the facts, read the story again.

OVERVIEW: SEQUENCE

Introducing the Skill

Remind students that when they read, the events or steps presented in a story have a special sequence. Explain that clue words, like *today, first, after, then, finally,* can help them find what happens first, next, and last in a story. Tell students that sequence can also be implied. Finding sequence without signal words means paying careful attention to verb tense. Another clue to implied sequence is the order in which information is presented. Students need to know that writers usually try to relate the events in a story in order. If there are no time signals, students can assume that events have occurred in the order in which they are presented.

How the Lessons Are Organized

A lesson consists of a reading selection about a single topic, followed by four questions. The first question asks students to put statements in order based on the information in each selection. The following questions ask about the stated or implied sequence in each selection.

Practice Activity

Read this story to your students.

Railroads Across America

It was 1862, and it was hard to get from East to West in America. Some people decided to build train tracks across the grasslands of America. One year later, workers began to build the tracks in the East. They laid tracks going toward the West. Two years later, workers in the West laid tracks going toward the East. Six years after the work started, the workers connected the tracks in Utah. Two trains came slowly down the tracks. One was from the East. One was from the West. East and West were joined at last!

Have students answer the following questions about the story.

1. Put these events in the order that they happened. What happened first?
   Two trains came slowly down the tracks. (second)
   The workers connected the tracks in Utah. (first)

2. When did people decide to build railroad tracks?
   A. before 1862
   <u>B. in 1862</u>
   C. after 1864

3. When did workers in the East begin?
   <u>A. before workers in the West</u>
   B. in early times
   C. in 1862

Explain to students that they should find words in the questions that are the same as words in the story, find the clue words in the story, and look at the order of the sentences.

OVERVIEW: CONTEXT

Introducing the Skill

Review this skill with students by using a simple cloze-type procedure. Ask students to supply the missing word in "The pretty, yellow ___ swam happily in the pond." Discuss how they know the word is *fish*. Remind students to pay attention to the meaning of surrounding words and phrases. Also, have them focus on language clues such as the position of the unknown or missing word in the sentence and what kind of words come before and after it.

How the Lessons Are Organized

A lesson consists of four reading selections. In lessons 1 through 6, the selections are presented in a cloze format with one or two missing words. In lessons 7 through 12, the selections contain a word in boldface type. Students are asked to use the context of the selection to choose the correct definition for each boldfaced word.

Practice Activity

Read this story to your students.

Birthday Parties

Not all birthday parties are ___. In one place in the world, everyone has a party on the same day. That day is New Year's Day. In another place, people don't get presents. Instead they give gifts to other people.

The word that best completes the sentence is ___.

   A. sad

   <u>B. alike</u>

   C. Monday

Remind students that to use context, they should read all the words in a story. Explain that if some words are too hard, they should continue reading, concentrating on all the words they know. When they try to find out what new words mean, tell them to look for words which go together. They should think of a meaning that goes with the other words in the story.

OVERVIEW: MAIN IDEA

Introducing the Skill

Have students recall a movie that they have recently seen. Ask them to state the plot of the movie using one sentence. Explain that this sentence is the main idea of the movie. Point out the difference between the main idea of the movie and the details that support the main idea. Stress that all of the details add up to the main idea.

How the Lessons Are Organized

A lesson consists of three or four short reading selections for which students are asked to identify the main idea.

Practice Activity

Read this story to your students.

> The Bill of Rights says that people are free to talk about anything. People can talk about things they like and don't like. The Bill of Rights is important in our lives. It helps us stay free.

The story mainly tells

    A. what kinds of things people say

    B. how people change bad things

    <u>C. what the Bill of Rights is about</u>

Remind students to ask themselves, "Is this sentence a main idea? Or is this sentence a detail?" Tell them to think about which sentence is bigger than all of the details.

OVERVIEW: CONCLUSION

Introducing the Skill

Emphasize that practicing this skill means thinking about what is actually stated in the reading selection. Ask students what they can conclude from the sentence, "Sylvia rushed into the kitchen and yanked the cookies from the smoking oven." Students can conclude that Sylvia was not in the kitchen before she pulled the cookies out of the oven. Point out that the sentence states that "Sylvia rushed into the kitchen." Students cannot conclude that Sylvia was baking the cookies, although they could infer this, because the sentence gives no evidence to support that conclusion. Perhaps another family member or friend was baking the cookies. Remind students that the conclusion they draw must be supported by the information in the selection in order to be a correct or logical conclusion.

How the Lessons Are Organized

Each lesson contains three or four short reading selections for which students are asked to choose a conclusion that can logically be drawn from the information presented.

Practice Activity

Read this story to your students.

How many times a day do you use wheels? If you ride in a car, you use wheels. That's plain to see. But there are many hidden wheels at home, too. A can opener has wheels with teeth. A fan is a wheel with blades.

From the story you can tell that

A. people use wheels ten times each day

B. people use wheels every day

C. can openers work just like cars

Remind students to read all the clues in the story. They should find a conclusion that fits all the clues. To make sure that they find the correct conclusion, ask, "How do I know this?" They should know because of the clues in the story.

OVERVIEW: INFERENCE

Introducing the Skill

Have students imagine that they are at a friend's house. Tell them there is a cake with candles on one table and many presents on another. Balloons and crepe-paper streamers hang from the ceiling. There are many people there. Ask students to make an inference about why this is a special day for their friend. Discuss what facts and personal knowledge or experiences lead them to infer that their friend is having a birthday party. Remind students that they can make inferences by thinking about what they already know and including it with the facts given in the reading selection. Point out that facts can be found in the selection but that the inference cannot.

How the Lessons Are Organized

A lesson consists of three or four short reading selections. All lessons ask students to choose one logical inference that can be made from the information presented in the selection.

Practice Activity

Read this story to your students.

> There was a knock at the front door. When June opened the door, she was surprised. Standing there was her friend Mark. He had come to bring her flowers.

Which of these sentences is probably true?

A. Mark brought candy for June.

B. June knew that Mark was coming.

C. Mark wanted to do something nice for June.

Remind students to read the story and to think about the facts presented. Then they should think about what they already know. Encourage them to make a guess by putting together what they know and what they read.

Dear Parent:

During this school year, our class will be working on a variety of reading skills. We will be completing activity sheets that provide practice in the comprehension skills that can help your child become a better reader. The skills we will be focusing on are: finding the facts, detecting a sequence, learning new vocabulary through context, identifying the main idea, drawing conclusions, and making inferences.

From time to time, I may send home activity sheets. To best help your child, please consider the following suggestions:

- Provide a quiet place to work.
- Go over the directions together.
- Encourage your child to do his or her best.
- Check the lesson when it is complete.
- Go over your child's work, and note improvements as well as problems.

Help your child maintain a positive attitude about reading. Provide as many opportunities for reading with your child as possible. Read books from the library, comics in the newspaper, and even cereal boxes. Let your child know that each lesson provides an opportunity to have fun and to learn. Above all, enjoy this time you spend with your child. He or she will feel your support, and skills will improve with each activity completed.

Thank you for your help!

Cordially,

Name_____   Date _____

Seashells

Read the story. Choose the answer that best completes the sentence.

Seashells come in many different shapes, sizes, and colors. Some shells grow as big as four feet long. The smallest shells are only half an inch long. Some shells have two sides that open like wings. Other shells are shaped like a curling tube. Shells come in all colors: white, black, brown, yellow, green, red, orange, and pink. They are like a rainbow in the ocean.

Many seashells are named for other things we know.
The spider shell is one example. The spider shell has long points that look like spider legs. The comb shell has points, too. Its points are straight and close together, just like those in a comb.

_____ **1.** Some shells grow
   A. rainbows
   B. four feet long
   C. butterfly wings

_____ **2.** The smallest shells are only
   A. half a foot long
   B. two inches wide
   C. half an inch long

_____ **3.** Some shells are named for
   A. people who found them
   B. other things we know
   C. where they are found

_____ **4.** Some seashells have
   A. arms
   B. points
   C. homes

Go on to the next page.

Name_____   Date _____

There are two kinds of bear shells. One is called the little bear. It is a small shell. The bear-paw shell is different. It is a big shell with two parts. Each half looks like an animal foot.

Some names of shells do not make any sense. The apple shell doesn't look like an apple at all. And the dog shell doesn't look like a dog. The butterfly shell is very plain. Many other shells look more like a butterfly than that one! But the heart shell does have the shape of a heart. Not all heart shells are red. Some are yellow. Others have brown spots.

_____ 5. There are
   A. two kinds of bear shells
   B. three types of butterflies
   C. two kinds of apple shells

_____ 6. The bear-paw shell has
   A. one part
   B. two parts
   C. three parts

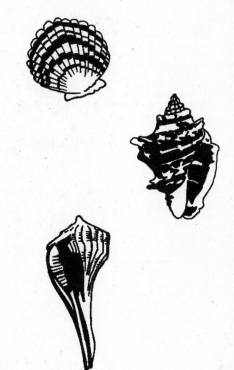

_____ 7. The dog shell
   A. looks like an animal foot
   B. doesn't look like a dog
   C. is yellow or red

_____ 8. Sometimes the heart shell has
   A. brown spots
   B. a butterfly shape
   C. three points

Name _____   **Date** _____

Old Glass Bottles

Read the story. Choose the answer that best completes the sentence.

Glass bottles were first made about three thousand years ago. The oldest bottles were made by hand. People blew them into different shapes. Long iron tubes were used to blow the glass. Each person used one tube. People dipped the tubes into melted glass. Then they blew through the tubes. Finally they broke the bottles off the tubes. The tubes left a mark on the finished glass. This mark shows that the glass was blown.

There are other ways to tell if a bottle was made by hand. The glass might have bubbles in it. The bubbles probably came from boiling the glass. Many times the bubbles would stay in the glass as it cooled.

_____ **1.** Glass bottles were first made
   A. three thousand years ago
   B. four hundred years ago
   C. one thousand years ago

_____ **2.** People made the oldest bottles
   A. out of wood
   B. with machines
   C. by hand

_____ **3.** To blow the glass, people used
   A. glass pots
   B. old bottles
   C. iron tubes

_____ **4.** Bubbles might come from
   A. soap
   B. breaking the glass
   C. boiling the glass

Go on to the next page.

Name _____   Date _____

Then people began making glass bottles other ways. They made bottles by pouring the glass into forms. It took two forms to make a bottle. There was one form for each half. Bottles made this way have lines down the sides. That's where the two halves were joined together.

Some old bottles have letters written in the glass. The letters are on the side or the bottom. You can feel them because they stick out. These letters tell the name of the bottle company. There are books that tell about the different companies. The books tell you when and where each bottle was made.

_____

_____ 5. People used other ways to
    A. make bottles
    B. blow glass
    C. write letters

_____ 6. Bottles with lines down the sides were
    A. blown with a new kind of tool
    B. broken and then fixed
    C. poured into two forms

_____ 7. Some bottles have letters on the
    A. inside of the bottle
    B. side or bottom
    C. top of the bottle

_____ 8. To find out when a bottle was made,
    A. use a book that tells about bottle companies
    B. learn to blow glass
    C. count the lines on the side of the glass

Name _____   Date _____

Our Amazing Skin

Read the story. Choose the answer that best completes the sentence.

Our skin is like a bag that we live in. Inside the bag our bodies are mostly water. Our water is like the water in the sea. It is very salty. Also like the ocean, we can lose our water. The wind and the sun could take it away. Our bag of skin keeps our body's ocean from drying up.

Our skin keeps out sunshine. Too much sun can hurt us. Skin also keeps out dirt. That's important because some kinds of dirt can make us sick. Our skin feels things. It feels warm things, cold things, things it touches, and things that hurt it. A campfire feels warm. A snowball thrown in our face feels cold and hurts. A hug is the touch of another person's skin on our own.

_____ 1. Our bodies are mostly
   A. salt
   B. water
   C. skin

_____ 2. Our skin keeps our body's water from
   A. drying up
   B. getting cold
   C. smelling bad

_____ 3. Skin keeps out
   A. dirt
   B. food
   C. water

_____ 4. Our skin helps us
   A. read
   B. feel
   C. dream

Go on to the next page.

Name _____   Date _____

Our hair is a special kind of covering. It helps keep things out of our eyes, ears, and nose. Hair is also good for keeping us warm. When we get goose bumps, our body hairs stand up. Then the hairs hold air close to our skin like a thin blanket. Hair keeps animals warm, too. Some animals have more hair than others. So they have a better blanket for cold weather.

Our nails are like very hard skin. They help keep our fingers and toes from getting hurt. Our nails aren't as strong or sharp as the nails that animals have. But they are good for scratching backs and picking up dimes.

_____ **5.** Hair helps keep things out of our
  A. fingers and toes
  B. mouth and ears
  C. eyes, ears, and nose

_____ **6.** Hair is good for
  A. keeping us clean
  B. helping us stay warm
  C. keeping us from getting hurt

_____ **7.** Nails are like
  A. flat hair
  B. hard skin
  C. thin blankets

_____ **8.** Nails help keep our
  A. toes sharp
  B. fingers from getting loose
  C. toes from getting hurt

Name_____   Date _____

Snowflake and Little Fish

Read the story. Choose the answer that best completes the sentence.

A tribe of people lived between a beautiful blue lake and a big white mountain. In this tribe lived twin sisters. Their names were Snowflake and Little Fish.

Life was good for the tribe. They had plenty of fish to eat from the lake. They had fresh water from the stream that came down the mountain. The people had everything they needed. But one year things changed. The days grew hot, even in the winter. No snow fell on the mountain. Without melting snow, the stream had no water. And without water from the stream, the lake became dry. Without water in the lake, the fish began to die.

_____ **1.** Snowflake and Little Fish were twin
    A. mountains
    B. brothers
    C. sisters

_____ **2.** The people of the tribe
    A. lived on a white mountain
    B. ate chicken in the summer
    C. had everything they needed

_____ **3.** One year the days were
    A. wet in the spring
    B. cold in the summer
    C. hot in the winter

_____ **4.** The fish began to
    A. jump
    B. die
    C. leave

Go on to the next page.

Name_____   **Date** _____

The women moaned. The men growled. The children cried. The people tried everything they could think of. But nothing worked. One evening Snowflake and Little Fish sat on a rock. They held hands and whispered together for a long time. Their faces were sad, but their eyes were bright. In the morning they were gone. One set of footprints went up the mountain. Another set of footprints went to the lake.

When the sun came up, the mountain was white with snow. Thousands of fish were jumping in the blue lake. The tribe was saved. But no one ever saw Snowflake and Little Fish again.

_____

_____ **5.** The men
  A. growled
  B. cried
  C. moaned

_____ **6.** Snowflake and Little Fish
  A. shouted, "Look at the mountain!"
  B. danced until the sun came up
  C. whispered for a long time

_____ **7.** One set of footprints went
  A. across the grass
  B. up the mountain
  C. to the fire

_____ **8.** When the sun came up, there were
  A. fish in the lake
  B. beautiful stars
  C. thousands of birds

Name_____ Date _____

Working Worms

Read the story. Choose the answer that best completes the sentence.

Many people feel that silk is the finest cloth of all. Just touching silk can be a surprise because it is so soft. Even more surprising is the fact that silk is made by special worms.

If you visited a silk farm, you would see two things: worms and trees. Silkworms eat only the leaves of mulberry trees. So rows and rows of these trees grow on silk farms. On some farms the leaves are picked by hand. Workers gather leaves from whole branches at once. In other places machines do this work. The farmers chop the leaves. Then they feed them to their worms.

_____ **1.** Silk is a type of very fine
  A. worm
  B. tree
  C. cloth

_____ **2.** At a silk farm, there are worms and
  A. spiders
  B. cows
  C. trees

_____ **3.** Silkworms eat only
  A. silk cloth
  B. mulberry leaves
  C. apple trees

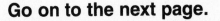

_____ **4.** On some farms the leaves are
  A. picked by hand
  B. cooked in pots
  C. left on trees

Go on to the next page.

Name _____   Date _____

Silkworms do nothing but sleep and eat. They grow very quickly. In just four weeks, they become ten thousand times heavier. As the worms grow, they shed their skin four times. The old skin splits and falls off.

After so much work, the worms are ready to change into moths. Each worm spins a single long thread around and around itself. This new home is called a cocoon. The thread of each cocoon is as thin as a spider's web. The farmers steam and dry the cocoons. Then the cocoons go to a silk-making plant. There the threads are spun into silk yarn. The yarn will be made into soft cloth that feels like a cloud.

_____ **5.** A silkworm grows
- **A.** slowly
- **B.** smaller
- **C.** quickly

_____ **6.** A silkworm's skin splits and
- **A.** gets smaller
- **B.** comes off
- **C.** becomes wet

_____ **7.** The thread of each cocoon is
- **A.** thin
- **B.** fat
- **C.** red

_____ **8.** Silk cloth is very
- **A.** rough
- **B.** tight
- **C.** soft

Name_____   Date _____

Hippos

Read the story. Choose the answer that best completes the sentence.

Hippos are animals that live in Africa. Their name means "river horse." But they do not look very much like horses. Hippos have large, round bodies. They have short legs and small ears. They look more like pigs than horses. In fact, hippos and pigs come from the same animal group.

Like pigs, hippos love mud. They stay cool under the hot sun by rolling in mud and swimming in rivers. In spite of their great size, hippos can swim fast. A hippo's eyes and nose stay above the water as it swims. If it dives under the water, it can stay there for as long as five minutes.

_____ **1.** A hippo's name means
    A. mud roller
    B. big diver
    C. river horse

_____ **2.** Hippos have
    A. no ears
    B. small ears
    C. big ears

_____ **3.** Hippos roll in mud to
    A. go to sleep
    B. stay cool
    C. get dirty

_____ **4.** A hippo can stay underwater for
    A. five minutes
    B. one day
    C. five hours

Go on to the next page.

Name_____   Date _____

A baby hippo can run and swim when it is born. It can get milk from its mother underwater. Baby hippos stay with their mother for years. When they go for a walk, the babies line up behind their mother. She leads them along like ducks.

Baby hippos love to play. They dive in the river and blow water from their noses. Sometimes they swim on top of their parents' backs or heads. But they cannot do this when they are grown. Grown hippos weigh as much as four tons.

_____ **5.** A baby hippo can
   A. fly
   B. talk
   C. swim

_____ **6.** Baby hippos stay with their mothers for
   A. months
   B. years
   C. weeks

_____ **7.** Hippos look like ducks when they
   A. start swimming
   B. are sleeping
   C. go for a walk

_____ **8.** Grown hippos can weigh up to
   A. four pounds
   B. four tons
   C. ten tons

Name_____   Date _____

The Name Game

Read the story. Choose the answer that best completes the sentence.

Years ago people had only one name. Each name had a special meaning. A baby might be given a name that meant "brave" or "bright." The parents hoped that the child would live up to the name. They thought that a good name would help the child.

Then towns got larger. Sometimes people with the same name lived close to one another. Their friends had to have a way to tell them apart. So people began to have longer names. The new names told something about the person.

_____ **1.** Years ago people had only one
   A. hat
   B. baby
   C. name

_____ **2.** Each name had
   A. a special meaning
   B. the same letters
   C. one correct spelling

_____ **3.** Sometimes people had
   A. too many names
   B. the same name
   C. two towns

_____ **4.** The new names told about the
   A. parents
   B. town
   C. person

Go on to the next page.

Sometimes the names told where a person lived. If there were two Johns, one might have been called John of the Woods. Maybe the other John had red hair. He would have been called John the Red.

By about the year 1300, most people had two names. They also started to give their names to their children. Many of these last names are still used today. Lincoln was a town in England. *Johnson* meant "son of John." Smiths were workers who used hammers. They worked with metal, wood, or stone.

_____ **5.** John the Red had
    A. red hair
    B. brown eyes
    C. black teeth

_____ **6.** By about 1300 people gave their children
    A. their own rooms
    B. more money
    C. two names

_____ **7.** Lincoln was a
    A. road
    B. town
    C. mountain

_____ **8.** Smiths worked with
    A. saws
    B. hammers
    C. knives

Name_____   Date _____

Elephants

Elephants are the largest mammals on land. Long ago there were elephants in most countries. Now elephants live only in Africa and Asia. They are smart animals who live together and help each other.

Female elephants live in close family groups. The group is made of mothers and their babies. The young males stay with this group until they are about 14 years old. Then they leave to join a group of male elephants. The males travel in groups, but they are not as close as the family groups. Males often move from one herd to another.

A herd wakes up at four in the morning. The elephants want to start grazing before it gets too hot. They walk to a water hole and drink. The herd walks and eats about 16 hours a day. They eat grass, leaves, bark, and fruit. Sometimes they stop and take naps. At midnight the herd stops for the night. All the elephants lie down and sleep. Some of them snore.

Babies can be born at any time of the year. A baby weighs 250 pounds when it is born. It stands up 15 minutes after it's born. The herd moves slowly for the first few days. The young one walks between its mother and another female. If it gets tired, they hold it up with their trunks. By the third day, the baby can keep up with the herd. At first the little one doesn't know how to use its trunk. Sometimes it steps on it. Sometimes it even sucks its trunk like a human baby sucks its thumb.

Go on to the next page.

Name_____   Date _____

1. Put these events in the order that they happened. What happened first? Write the number **1** on the line by that sentence. Then write the number **2** by the sentence that tells what happened next.

_____ Elephants live only in Africa and Asia.

_____ Elephants lived in most countries.

Choose the phrase that best answers the question.

_____ **2.** When do young males join a male herd?
   A. when they are about 14
   B. in the early morning
   C. when their mothers tell them to

_____ **3.** When does a herd wake up?
   A. after it gets hot
   B. at midnight
   C. about four in the morning

_____ **4.** When are baby elephants born?
   A. in the spring
   B. during any season
   C. usually in the summer

Name _____ Date _____

The Dai Family, Americans

The Dai family had been living in America for five years. One night Mrs. Dai said, "We must talk about something. We left Vietnam in fear. We had to run and hide. At last we came to America. No one tries to hurt us here. Now we have the chance to be Americans. But if we become Americans, we will no longer be Vietnamese. What should we do?" The Dais talked for a long time.

Then Mr. Dai said, "I'm proud that I was born in Vietnam. But the country we loved is not there anymore. We can't go back. It would be good if we became Americans."

One bright Saturday Mr. Dai went to the library and got some books. He asked the children for help. They had been going to school. They helped their parents learn to read English. The Dais read about how Americans choose their president.

Then the Dais took some tests. Next the Dais filled out some papers. People checked the papers. They also checked to make sure the Dais had not broken any laws. After a month the family got a letter from a judge. He wanted to see them on Monday. On that day they put on their best clothes and went to the judge. First the judge asked Mr. and Mrs. Dai if they would follow the laws. They both said they would. Next the judge

had them raise their right hands. They said they would be true to America. The judge said, "You are now Americans."

Go on to the next page.

Name _____   Date _____

1. Put these events in the order that they happened. What happened first? Write the number **1** on the line by that sentence. Then write the number **2** by the sentence that tells what happened next.

_____ The Dais took some tests.

_____ The Dais filled out papers.

Choose the phrase that best answers the question.

_____ 2. When did Mr. and Mrs. Dai learn to read English?

    A. while they lived in Vietnam

    B. after the judge said they were Americans

    C. before they went to see the judge

_____ 3. When did the judge see the Dais?

    A. on Monday

    B. on Wednesday

    C. one bright Saturday

_____ 4. What did the judge ask the Dais first?

    A. if they would raise their right hands

    B. if they promised to follow the laws

    C. if they promised to be true to America

Name _____   Date _____

Sky-Father-in-Heaven

Some Native Americans tell this story. It is about how they think the world began.

Long, long ago, Sky-Father-in-Heaven was alone. He had no one to be his friend. So he decided to make some new things.

Sky-Father rolled a piece of dark night into a ball. He looked at the ball with his big eyes. It began to shine with a bright light. "This will be the sun," Sky-Father said. He put the sun high in the sky. He then made little balls of night. He looked at the balls, and they also began to shine. He made these the stars.

Next Sky-Father took another ball of night. He held it close to his heart. This ball of night became the earth. Then Sky-Father cried. His tears filled up all the seas. He put the earth near the sun. Grass and trees grew on the earth.

But Sky-Father was still lonely. He took yellow clay from the earth. He made a yellow man. Then he made a black man from black earth. He mixed sand with water and made a white man. Next he took more dirt and made a red man and a brown man. He baked the five men in an oven. When he took them out, they were not made of dirt anymore. He put his hands on the men, and they came to life. At last Sky-Father took wind, water, and dirt. He made First Woman from these. Then Sky-Father put the five men and First Woman on the earth. He wasn't lonely anymore.

Go on to the next page.

Name_____   Date _____

1. Put these events in the order that they happened. What happened first? Write the number **1** on the line by that sentence. Then write the number **2** by the sentence that tells what happened next.

_____ Sky-Father's tears filled the seas.

_____ Sky-Father held a ball of night to his heart.

Choose the phrase that best answers the question.

_____ **2.** When did Sky-Father make the stars?
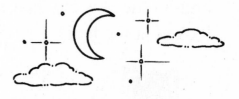
  A. before he made the men
  B. before he made the sun
  C. after he made the earth

_____ **3.** When did Sky-Father make the earth?

  A. after he made First Woman
  B. after he made the men
  C. after he made the sun and stars

_____ **4.** When did Sky-Father make a brown man?

  A. before he made a yellow man
  B. after he made First Woman
  C. after he made a black man

Name _____   Date _____

A Cowboy's Day

It was a cool spring morning. The cook shouted, "Everyone up! Get your food before I throw it out!" The sleeping cowboys woke up and stretched. They went to the cook's wagon for breakfast.

All winter the cattle had been out in the fields. They ran wild and ate grass. But now the owners wanted to see how many cattle they had. So the cowboys had to find the cattle and catch them. They called this rounding up the cattle.

After breakfast the men got on their best horses and rode away. Soon they found some cattle in a field. The cowboys rode around the herd. Then they started moving the cattle. The animals were afraid, and some didn't want to go. But the cowboys kept them moving. Finally they got to a big, wooden pen.

Then the cowboys looked at the cattle. Some of the cattle had a mark burned into their hair. The marks showed who owned the cattle. But the young cows didn't have any marks. They had been born just that winter. When a cowboy saw a calf without a mark, he caught it with a rope. He knew who owned the calf because each mother cow had a mark. The calf had to be given the same mark the mother cow had. The cowboys pressed a hot iron into the calf's fur.

Soon all the calves were marked. Late that night the cowboys would have a little party. They would joke, sing, and tell stories.

Go on to the next page.

Name_____

Date _____

1. Put these events in the order that they happened. What happened first? Write the number **1** on the line by that sentence. Then write the number **2** by the sentence that tells what happened next.

_____ The men caught calves with a rope.

_____ The cowboys looked at the cattle.

Choose the phrase that best answers the question.

_____ **2.** When were the cattle brought to the pen?

    A. after the cowboys found the cattle

    B. when the cook shouted

    C. after the cowboys had a party

_____ **3.** When did the cowboys put marks on the cattle?

    A. before they ate breakfast in the morning

    B. when they first found them in the field

    C. when the cattle got to the big pen

_____ **4.** When did the cowboys have a party?

    A. before all the calves had been marked

    B. late at night

    C. when they ate breakfast

Name_____   Date _____

Coming to America

"Anton sent a letter from America!" Mrs. Novak cried. "Stan, will you read it to us?" Stan read the letter. It said: "I have found work that pays well. I have meat three times a week. But I miss you. Here is money to pay for Stan to come over. He and I will work hard and save our money. Then you, my dear parents, can come. With great love and hope, Anton."

The next day Mrs. Novak put Stan's clothes in a bag. She put bread, cheese, and dry meat in a basket. Mr. Novak said, "Go with our blessing. Love your new land. But do not forget Poland." Then Stan walked the thirty miles to the sea.

At last Stan got on a big boat. He did not have much money, so he stayed in a large room with many people. People slept on shelves. There were no beds. It was very crowded, and it smelled bad. Sometimes high waves made the boat rock. Sometimes Stan got sick from the rocking. The trip lasted six long weeks.

One cloudy day someone shouted, "Land! We are here at last!" Stan ran to look. Some people were so happy they cried.

The boat came to an island. Then people got off and stood in long lines. Doctors looked at them to see if they were healthy. Other people asked many questions. They asked, "Have you broken laws? Can you work?" At last Stan was sent to a small boat that took him off the island and to the mainland. Then Stan began the walk to Anton's home and to his new life.

Go on to the next page.

Name _____   Date _____

1. Put these events in the order that they happened. What happened first? Write the number **1** on the line by that sentence. Then write the number **2** by the sentence that tells what happened next.

_____ Stan Novak got on the boat in Poland.

_____ Anton Novak wrote to his family in Poland.

Choose the phrase that best answers the question.

_____ 2. When did Stan Novak walk thirty miles?
   A. after he got to America
   B. after he got sick on the boat
   C. before he got to the big boat

_____ 3. When did people ask Stan many questions?
   A. before his family got the letter
   B. before he got on the big boat
   C. after he landed on the island

_____ 4. When did Stan walk to Anton's home?
   A. before people asked him many questions
   B. after a small boat took him off of the island
   C. during the long boat trip on the sea

Name_____   Date _____

The Brothers Grimm

You know who Snow White is. You've heard of Hansel and Gretel. But have you heard of the Brothers Grimm? If not for them, you might never have heard these tales.

Jakob and Wilhelm Grimm were the oldest of six children. Jakob was born in 1785. Wilhelm was born the next year. They were the best of friends. The brothers lived and worked together for most of their lives.

In 1798 the Grimms moved to the town of Cassel. There they finished school. Then they found jobs in the king's library. Both men loved old stories. In their free time, they searched for old folktales and songs.

From 1807 to 1814, Jakob and Wilhelm collected tales from everyone they knew. Marie Muller was a nanny. She told them the tales of *Snow White*, *Little Red Riding Hood*, and *Sleeping Beauty*. One day the Grimms met Frau Viehmann. She came to their house many times. She drank coffee and ate rolls. She told the Grimms more than twenty tales. *Cinderella* was one of them.

In 1812 the Grimms' first book of fairy tales was published. The Grimms had meant the stories for grown-ups. They were surprised when children loved them, too. They wanted to find more tales. This time it was much easier. Now people would bring stories to them. The next book of tales was published in 1815. The last book of *Grimm's Fairy Tales* was published in 1857.

Go on to the next page.

Name_____   Date _____

1. Put these events in the order that they happened. What happened first? Write the number **1** on the line by that sentence. Then write the number **2** by the sentence that tells what happened next.

_____ The brothers finished school.

_____ The brothers collected tales.

Choose the phrase that best answers the question.

_____ 2. When was Wilhelm Grimm born?
   A. the year before Jakob was born
   B. in 1785
   C. the year after Jakob was born

_____ 3. When did the brothers collect tales from friends?
   A. from 1807 to 1814
   B. in 1798
   C. when they were children

_____ 4. When was the Grimms' first book of fairy tales published?
   A. when the brothers were in school
   B. after they began working in the library
   C. from 1807 to 1814

Name _____   Date _____

The Great White Bear

In some languages they are called snow bears or ice bears. We call them polar bears. These giants live in the arctic lands of the far north. Only a few creatures are strong enough to live in such a cold, empty place. Polar bears live alone except when a mother bear has cubs. Female bears have cubs every three years. Like most bears, they are good mothers.

Polar bears mate in April. In September the female goes back to the place she was born. She looks for a den. In December the mother gives birth to two cubs. The cubs are smaller than human babies. And they are just as helpless.

By March the cubs weigh 25 pounds. It is time for them to see the world. They leave the den. At first they are cold and puzzled. They slip and slide as they try to walk on the ice.

Later in the spring, the mother leads the cubs to the seashore. They must catch seals before the ice melts and the seals leave. The cubs walk in their mother's tracks. She teaches them to sniff the air for food. Polar bears can smell food as far as ten miles away.

When they arrive at the seashore, she teaches them how to catch seals. She shows them how to swim in the icy water. When they are two years old, the cubs leave their mother. She has taught them everything they need to know to live on their own.

Go on to the next page.

Name _____   Date _____

1. Put these events in the order that they happened. What happened first? Write the number **1** on the line by that sentence. Then write the number **2** by the sentence that tells what happened next.

_____ The mother and cubs stay in the den until March.

_____ The female bear returns to the place she was born.

Choose the phrase that best answers the question.

_____ **2.** When do polar bears mate?

    A. usually in April

    B. when they are two years old

    C. in September

_____ **3.** When are the cubs born?

    A. later in the spring

    B. in December

    C. when the mother arrives at the seashore

_____ **4.** When do the cubs leave their mother?

    A. when they come out of the den

    B. when they are three months old

    C. after they learn to catch seals

Name _____   Date _____

Read the story. Choose the word or phrase that best completes the sentence.

1. Jumping beans _____ because a worm lives inside. The worm lies still when it is cool. But when it gets warm, the worm moves around. Hold a jumping bean in your hand. The heat from your hand will make the worm move. And that makes the bean jump.

_____   The word that best completes the sentence is
          A. hear   **B.** hop   **C.** push

---

2. Look at the stars. They are different colors. The color tells how hot a star is. The hottest stars are blue. White stars are not quite as hot as blue ones. Then come yellow stars, like our sun. They are even _____ than white stars. The coldest stars are the red ones. But even red stars are too hot to visit.

_____   The word that best completes the sentence is
          A. cooler   **B.** brighter   **C.** better

---

3. People aren't the only creatures that use tools. Many animals use tools, too. Some monkeys use sticks to catch ants. A monkey pokes a stick into an ant bed. The _____ get angry and bite the stick. Then the monkey pulls the stick out and eats the ants. Ants use tools, too. They make little wagons from leaves. They use the leaves to carry food back to their ant beds.

_____   The word that best completes the sentence is
          A. flies   **B.** insects   **C.** aunts

---

4. Most puppets are just toys. But a famous painter named Paul Klee made puppets that were art. Klee used strange and unusual things to make his puppets. One puppet had a head made from a pine cone. Another one had a shell nose. Some puppets wore _____ made out of wire and clothes made out of strings.

_____   The word that best completes the sentence is
          A. books   **B.** dogs   **C.** hats

Go on to the next page.

Name_____   Date _____

5. Juliette Gordon Low started the Girl Scouts in America. She had heard about the Boy Scouts. She thought it would be a good idea for girls, too. She believed that girls should learn more than just cooking. They should **explore** the outdoors and take care of themselves while doing so. In 1912 there were 18 Girl Scouts. Now there are 3 million Girl Scouts!

_____   In this story the word **explore** means
A. walk   B. search   C. paint

6. On New Year's Day in China, there is a parade. People dress up and march down the street. A **special** part is the Lion Dance. The lion in the dance is not a real lion. Two people wear a lion suit. One person is the head. The other person is the body. Together they make the lion run, jump, paw the air, and wag its tail.

_____   In this story the word **special** means
A. important   B. necessary   C. happy

7. Cars burn gas in order to go. People burn food instead. You burn about two teaspoons of sugar when you walk a mile. But if you ride a bike, you can **extend** the distance. You can go five miles on two teaspoons of sugar! The wheels do the work instead of your feet.

_____   In this story the word **extend** means
A. double   B. makes longer C. makes shorter

8. Cats and owls can see at night. But no animal can see in **complete** darkness. People and animals see because of light coming into their eyes. Some animals, like cats and owls, can see in very little light. The light can be so dim that people can't see at all.

_____   In this story the word **complete** means
A. between   B. little   C. all

Name_____   Date _____

Read the story. Choose the word or phrase that best completes the sentence.

1. When Philip was a boy, settlers came to live near his tribe. Philip's father was chief then. He and the settlers made a peace _____ . Later, Philip became chief. He was called King Philip. He was upset with the settlers. They had built their homes on the tribe's land. King Philip started a war with the settlers. He was killed in the war. The tribe lost its land forever.

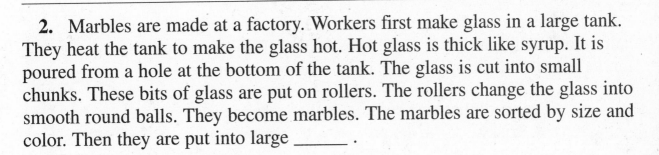

_____   The word that best completes the sentence is
     A. sand   **B.** color   **C.** treaty

---

2. Marbles are made at a factory. Workers first make glass in a large tank. They heat the tank to make the glass hot. Hot glass is thick like syrup. It is poured from a hole at the bottom of the tank. The glass is cut into small chunks. These bits of glass are put on rollers. The rollers change the glass into smooth round balls. They become marbles. The marbles are sorted by size and color. Then they are put into large _____ .

_____   The word that best completes the sentence is
     A. bins   **B.** friends   **C.** stars

---

3. An underground cave can have a stream in it. A cave fish lives in this stream. The fish is small and white. It can't see because it doesn't have any _____ . It doesn't need them since there is no light in the cave. The cave fish finds food by smell and feel.

_____   The word that best completes the sentence is
     A. arms   **B.** eyes   **C.** teeth

---

4. Mangrove trees grow in salt water. Most trees take in water with their roots. Then they let it out through their leaves. When mangroves take in water, they take in salt, too. They let the water and the salt out. After that, mangroves look as if someone _____ salt all over their leaves.

_____   The word that best completes the sentence is
     A. threw   **B.** liked   **C.** grew

Name_____   Date _____

Read the story. Choose the word or phrase that best completes the sentence.

1. Death Valley is in California. There is a very old, dry lake bed there. It is called the Racetrack. Marks on the ground show that large rocks there have moved. Some people think that the rocks move because of the weather. When it rains there, the dirt gets muddy. Then strong winds blow the rocks over the _____ ground. The rocks leave marks in the mud. After the mud dries, the marks can still be seen.

_____   The word that best completes the sentence is
A. beautiful   B. foolish   C. slippery

2. Gerbils are small, furry creatures. They have long back legs and a long, hairy tail. Gerbils are _____ and love to play. They are easy to care for and fun to watch. That is why gerbils make such good pets.

_____   The word that best completes the sentence is
A. frisky   B. lazy   C. sleepy

3. People have taken over much of the land. Many wild creatures have lost their homes. Some people worry about this. A few of them formed a group. The group is called the World Wildlife Fund. This group works to save animals and their homes. Many animals live in the rain _____ . The World Wildlife Fund works to keep the trees there from being cut down.

_____   The word that best completes the sentence is
A. drops   B. beds   C. forests

4. Juan Largo has spent seven years learning about black bears. He catches the bears. Then he puts little radios on them. He can track the bears and _____ down what they do. He even knows where they sleep during the winter. Sometimes he puts a tag on a bear's ear. Then he will know that bear when he sees it again.

_____   The word that best completes the sentence is
A. back   B. write   C. sing

Name_____   Date _____

Read the story. Choose the word or phrase that best completes the sentence.

1.   There are different ways to show what the world looks like. One way is a map. A map is a flat drawing of the world. Another way to show the world is a _____ . This shows that the world is round.

_____   The word that best completes the sentence is
        A. sandwich   **B.** flash   **C.** globe

_____

2.   People who work with metal are called welders. They join pieces of metal together. Welders use _____ to make the metal hot. They melt the edges of the pieces and join them together. When the pieces cool, they stay together. Welders always have to think about safety when they work. They wear special clothes so they won't be hurt.

_____   The word that best completes the sentence is
        A. flashlights **B.** torches   **C.** scissors

_____

3.   A parrot is a bird that can talk. It copies the sounds it hears. This bird has special _____ in its neck. The parrot tightens and loosens them. That's how it makes the sounds it hears. A wild parrot sounds like other parrots. But a pet parrot can bark like a dog, ring like a phone, or talk like a person. A pet parrot can even sing and whistle.

_____   The word that best completes the sentence is
        A. candy   **B.** bottles   **C.** muscles

_____

4.   A young girl was taken from her home and made a slave. She was brought to the United States and sold. The Wheatley family bought her. Her name was changed to Phillis Wheatley. Her new family taught her how to read and write. Phillis started writing poems. Later she was freed. She once sent a poem to George Washington. He _____ her poem very much. He asked Phillis to visit him.

_____   The word that best completes the sentence is
        A. admired   **B.** wore   **C.** rode

Name _____   Date _____

Read the story. Choose the word or phrase that best completes the sentence.

1. A beaver's house is called a lodge. The lodge is built on a pond or a river. It is made with branches and twigs. The beaver enters the lodge from a tunnel under the water. Inside the lodge is a room. The _____ of the room is above the water. The beaver can dry off and stay warm in the room of its lodge.

_____ The word that best completes the sentence is
     A. floor   **B.** knee   **C.** shoe

2. Charles Drew was good in sports. He wanted to teach others how to play sports. So he became a _____ . Later, Charles went back to school. He wanted to be a doctor. While in school Charles studied about blood. He found a way to store blood. Then it could be used when it was needed. Many people's lives were saved. Charles won many awards for his work.

_____ The word that best completes the sentence is
     A. pilot   **B.** dancer   **C.** coach

3. Mount St. Helens is a volcano. It is in the state of Washington. It was quiet for almost fifty years. Then one day Mount St. Helens exploded. Ash was thrown into the air. Lava flowed, and hot rocks flew out. Melting snow caused floods. Forests caught on fire. The _____ where people stayed were burned. Some people lost their lives.

_____ The word that best completes the sentence is
     A. cabins   **B.** meals   **C.** nights

4. A shooting star looks like a streak of light in the sky. It's a piece of metal or stone called a meteor. It passes through the air around the earth. It gets very hot. It gets so hot that it glows. Sometimes there are many in the sky at once. It looks as if it's raining shooting stars. This is called a meteor _____.

_____ The word that best completes the sentence is
     A. television   **B.** shower   **C.** zoo

Name _____   Date _____

Read the story. Choose the word or phrase that best completes the sentence.

1.   A rodeo is great fun. It reminds us of what life was like for cowboys in the Old West. Men and women try to win prizes at a rodeo. They can choose to be in many kinds of _____ . Some people like to ride a wild horse or a bull. Others like to rope a calf or throw a steer onto its back.

_____   The word that best completes the sentence is
    A. grass   **B.** islands   **C.** contests

---

2.   The wart hog is a type of pig that lives in Africa. The wart hog is a light gray color. It has short, stiff hairs on its body. It also has a _____ of longer hair that runs down its neck. The hog has a large head that is flat in front. It has long, curved teeth, or tusks. The hog gets its name from the three pairs of bumps on its head, called warts.

_____   The word that best completes the sentence is
    A. basket   **B.** mane   **C.** party

---

3.   Long ago, people rushed west to hunt for gold. They lived in _____ near gold mines. Then they built homes. Soon whole towns grew up near the mines. But many of these towns didn't last long. When people had found all of the gold, they went to a new place. The towns they left behind became ghost towns. Only the empty buildings and streets were left.

_____   The word that best completes the sentence is
    A. camps   **B.** chairs   **C.** dollars

---

4.   The day lily is a plant. It has _____ without leaves. At the end of each one is a group of flowers. These flowers are yellow or orange. During the summer two or three of them bloom each day. They bloom when the sun comes up. Then they die when the sun sets.

_____   The word that best completes the sentence is
    A. fences   **B.** apartments   **C.** stalks

Name_____   Date _____

Read the story. Choose the word or phrase that best completes the sentence.

1. A cat's tongue feels rough. This is true for all cats. House cats, lions, and tigers all have rough tongues. A cat uses its tongue in many ways. It _____ itself to brush its fur. The cat removes dirt and loose hair this way. The cat also uses its rough tongue to scrape meat from a bone. When the cat is through, the bone is clean.

_____   The word that best completes the sentence is
    A. paints   **B.** licks   **C.** frightens

---

2. Trees are important. People make many things from trees. Trees are also helpful. They hold the dirt in place and help make the air we breathe. Trees are also the home for many creatures. So we need to be sure we _____ the trees. When old trees are cut down, new ones must be planted.

_____   The word that best completes the sentence is
    A. forget   **B.** find   **C.** save

---

3. Young people can join the Four-H Club. The goal of this club is to improve head, heart, hands, and health. Members have a chance to learn skills. They also find out about careers. Members try out jobs by working on _____. These jobs might deal with plants, animals, food, or safety.

_____   The word that best completes the sentence is
    A. ice   **B.** moments   **C.** projects

---

4. A barnyard pig takes a bath in mud. This is not because it likes to be dirty. In fact it would like cool, clean water much better. But a pig must find a way to cool off. It can't _____ to stay cool the way people do. So it will lie in the mud to stay cool. The thick mud also helps the pig's skin. Insects can't bite it, and the sun won't burn it.

_____   The word that best completes the sentence is
    A. fly   **B.** sweat   **C.** kick

Comprehension 3, SV 6185-0

Name_____   Date _____

Read the story. Choose the word or phrase that best completes the sentence.

1. Some snakes have four eyes. They have eyes that see in the day. But they also have two more eyes. These eyes can see heat. Snakes use these eyes to look for food. A snake **gazes** all around with its special eyes. Its eyes cannot see a plant. Plants do not give off any heat. But the eyes can see a mouse. A mouse is warm and good for snakes to eat.

_____   In this story the word **gazes** means

    A. stares   **B.** gives   **C.** adds

---

2. Deep inside, the earth is made of very hot rock. The rock is so hot that it can turn water into steam. In some places this steam comes out of cracks in the ground. In other places people pipe the steam up from deep in the ground. People use this steam **energy** to warm their homes.

_____   In this story the word **energy** means

    A. ice   **B.** power   **C.** stream

---

3. What is vegetable art? Ask Bob Spohn. For fifty years Spohn has **whittled** faces and animals out of large vegetables. He uses a knife to make the faces. Then he paints them. He once made a smiling face from a giant pumpkin. The pumpkin was almost a yard high and weighed 110 pounds!

_____   In this story the word **whittled** means

    A. drawn   **B.** shaken   **C.** cut

---

4. You spill a drink on your clothes. What do you do? First find some club soda. Rub it on your clothes where the **stain** is. Dry your clothes with a towel. The spot should be gone.

_____   In this story the word **stain** means

    A. mark   **B.** button   **C.** machine

Name_____   Date _____

Read the story. Choose the word or phrase that best completes the sentence.

1. Bluebirds are pretty birds. Their head and wings are bright blue. Most bluebirds have some red on their chest. The bluebird's song is sweet. People are worried about this small bird. There used to be many of them in towns and forests. Now bluebirds are becoming very **rare**.

_____   In this story the word **rare** means
      A. hard to find **B.** mean   **C.** fun to catch

2. Most people think sea birds live only near the sea. But **numerous** sea birds fly toward land, too. In the spring and summer, they go to rivers and lakes to nest. They go to the same place every year.

_____   In this story the word **numerous** means
      A. troubled   **B.** sick   **C.** many

3. Itzhak Perlman is a great violin player. As a boy he heard beautiful music on the radio. When he was just three years old, he **requested** a violin. He wanted to play beautiful music, too. At first his parents bought him a toy violin. But he knew it did not sound right. So they bought him a real one. Now he plays the violin all over the world.

_____   In this story the word **requested** means
      A. took away **B.** asked for   **C.** got back

4. There is a bird that can swim underwater and climb trees. It has claws on its wings. These birds build their nests over rivers and lakes. Sometimes the baby birds are afraid of other animals. Then they dive into the water and swim to another tree. They use their wing claws to climb up to a high branch. These birds use many tricks to **outwit** their enemies.

_____   In this story the word **outwit** means
      A. corner   **B.** attack   **C.** fool

Name_____ Date _____

Read the story. Choose the word or phrase that best completes the sentence.

1. You may not know Clara Barton's name. You know her work, though. She started the American Red Cross. During the Civil War, Barton went to battles to help wounded soldiers. After the war she saw that many soldiers could not find their families. She started to **trace** the missing people. Later she learned about the Red Cross in Europe. She decided that the United States needed a Red Cross, too.

_____   In this story the word **trace** means
          A. mail   **B.** teach   **C.** find

_____

2. In the ocean, waves look like moving mountains. But when they get close to a beach, they begin to fall over. Why does this happen? Close to the shore the water is **shallow**. The waves that come from the deep sea are very tall. Then they get close to shore. They try to stand tall, but they fall over.

_____   In this story the word **shallow** means
          A. not slow   **B.** not deep   **C.** not salty

_____

3. Benny Goodman was a band leader. He was called the King of Swing. His band played music that had a new sound. This swing music was **snappy**. It had a strong beat. People danced a fast new dance to this music. It was also called the swing.

_____   In this story the word **snappy** means
          A. tall   **B.** gray   **C.** quick

_____

4. Not all sharks are mean. Nurse sharks look bad, but they almost never hurt people. Instead they stay on the bottom of the ocean. They swim along, **sucking** in sand, crabs, snails, and tiny fish. They spit out the sand and eat the animals!

_____   In this story the word **sucking** means
          A. rolling   **B.** pulling   **C.** calling

Name_____   Date _____

Read the story. Choose the word or phrase that best completes the sentence.

1. The first jigsaw puzzle was made in England. It was made by a teacher. The teacher wanted his students to learn about the map of England. He **glued** a map to a sheet of wood. Then he cut the map along county lines. The students loved working the puzzle. They learned all about the map of England.

_____   In this story the word **glued** means
    A. served   **B.** dressed   **C.** pasted

2. Squanto was a Native American. He was taken to Spain as a slave. But he ran away to England. Then Squanto sailed back to his home. He met the Pilgrims living at Plymouth. They were **nearly** dead. They had no food. Squanto helped the Pilgrims. He taught them how to plant corn. He showed them where to fish and hunt.

_____   In this story the word **nearly** means
    A. tomorrow   **B.** almost   **C.** soon

3. Most wild animals have color in their fur or skin. But some do not. These animals are called albinos. They are white or very **pale**. Their white color makes them easy to see. Albinos can't sneak up on smaller animals. They also can't hide. So they die or become food for others.

_____   In this story the word **pale** means
    A. light   **B.** dark   **C.** happy

4. Neon is a type of gas found in the air. It is used in some **lamps** for homes and businesses. It is used to fill tubes for store signs, too. Now artists have found a new way to use neon. They make pictures with the neon-filled tubes. When the pictures are done, they are plugged in. People are amazed by the bright colors in neon art.

HOBBY SHOP

_____   In this story the word **lamps** means
    A. barns   **B.** coats   **C.** lights

Name_____   Date _____

Read the story. Choose the word or phrase that best completes the sentence.

1. You may not see many wild animals during the day. But there is a way to tell where wild animals have been. You can look for their tracks. Tracks are the prints their feet leave on the ground. You can **determine** which wild creatures left the tracks. The size and shape of the tracks will give you clues.

_____   In this story the word **determine** means
   A. speak **B.** repair **C.** tell

2. Waves often wash pretty shells up on the beach. But shells are not the only **appealing** things the waves bring. Sea beans are also washed up on shore. They are seeds and fruits from distant lands. They can be found on the beach from late March through the first part of summer.

_____   In this story the word **appealing** means
   A. brave **B.** interesting **C.** ugly

3. Maya Lin drew a design for a contest. Her design won and was built. Thousands of names were carved on two walls of shiny, black stone. The names were Americans who had died in the Vietnam War. At first people thought that the stone was ugly. They **disliked** it. But then they began to change their minds. They found that they could walk up to the walls. They could touch the names of loved ones.

_____   In this story the word **disliked** means
   A. lost **B.** tricked **C.** hated

4. Bobwhites are birds that live in groups. They search for insects and seeds in the woods. If the bobwhites come to a **clearing**, they run across it. They want to get back to the safety of the woods as fast as they can. At night these birds form a circle before they go to sleep. This helps them stay warm. They can also fly off in all directions if there's any danger.

_____   In this story the word **clearing** means
   A. river **B.** field **C.** mountain

Name_____   Date _____

Read the story. Choose the word or phrase that best completes the sentence.

1. Roller-coaster cars are hooked to a chain at first. A motor on the ground runs the chain. It pulls the cars to the top of the first hill. Then the cars are unhooked. When the cars roll down hill, they speed up. The cars slow down as they **coast** up the next hill. They speed up again as they go down it. Each hill is a bit lower than the last. The cars can't go up a hill that is as high as the one they just came down.

_____   In this story the word **coast** means

    A. move   **B.** park   **C.** leak

---

2. Stevie Wonder was born blind. This did not stop him from using his talent. He found that he was good with music. He learned how to play many instruments. He wrote his own songs. At the age of twelve, he sang his first hit. Since then he has made many **albums**. He has even written music for a movie.

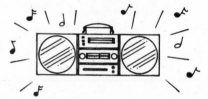

_____   In this story the word **albums** means

    A. oranges   **B.** buttons   **C.** records

---

3. Some people tell stories about Bunyips. Bunyips are said to live in lakes and rivers. There are many kinds of these strange beasts. Some are part person and part fish. Others look like big, brown creatures. They are **shaggy** and have big mouths. Still others look like dogs with webbed feet.

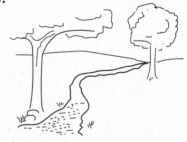

_____   In this story the word **shaggy** means

    A. hairy   **B.** silly   **C.** empty

---

4. The Great Salt Lake is in Utah. It used to be large. But it gets smaller each year. Homes that people built on the shore are now far from the water. This has happened because it is so hot and dry. The water dries up or **soaks** into the ground. There's not enough fresh water to make up for this loss.

_____   In this story the word **soaks** means

    A. feels   **B.** sinks   **C.** ties

Name _____   Date _____

Read the story. Choose the answer that best completes the sentence.

1. Baseball teams buy new balls for big games. But the new balls are slippery. So before each game, someone puts mud on them. But it's a special kind of mud. It makes the balls easier to use.

_____ The story mainly tells
   A. why ball players put mud on new balls
   B. where the baseball mud comes from
   C. when mud takes care of problems

2. Baby frogs grow from eggs. How? The mother frog lays her eggs in a pond. The dark center of each egg grows a tail. The eggs have no shells, so the young frog soon starts wiggling around. The baby frog looks like a fish. It swims with its tail and eats tiny water plants. Later it grows four legs and loses its tail. It learns to live both on land and in water.

_____ The story mainly tells
   A. how frogs grow from eggs
   B. why eggs have dark centers
   C. what eats tiny water plants

3. For a long time, sailors have known that sea plants help heal cuts or sores. Now someone has made sea plants into a kind of bandage. It keeps dirt out of skin cuts. It also helps cuts heal.

_____ The story mainly tells
   A. how sea water keeps dirt out of cuts
   B. why sailors are always hurting themselves
   C. how sea plants are used to heal cuts

4. Look at the back of a dollar bill. You will find a circle with an eagle in it. That is the Great Seal of the United States. What do the parts of the seal stand for? The eagle is a strong bird. It stands for might. The bird holds a branch and some arrows. The branch stands for peace. The arrows stand for war. The eagle has a ribbon in its mouth. The writing on the ribbon says, "Out of many states, one nation."

_____ The story mainly tells
   A. what is on the front of a dollar bill
   B. what the parts of the Great Seal stand for
   C. what the ribbon on the dollar says   **Go on to the next page.**

Name_____   Date _____

5. It's easy to go up in a hot-air balloon. It's harder to come down. A gas burner heats the air inside a hot-air balloon. The hot air rises. So does the balloon. But what if people in the balloon want to come down? They have to wait for the air in the balloon to cool. Then the balloon slowly falls. They throw out ropes. Then the balloon is pulled to the ground.

_____   The story mainly tells

    A. how hot-air balloons go up and down

    B. who rides hot-air balloons

    C. when a hot-air balloon needs air

6. People can almost fly like birds. To do this, they fly planes called gliders. Gliders have no engines. All the pilot hears is the rush of the wind. Warm air keeps the gliders up. As the air rises, it takes the glider with it. To find warm air, pilots watch for birds. Birds like to glide in warm air, too.

_____   The story mainly tells

    A. how birds glide in the wind

    B. how warm air can be

    C. how people can fly like birds

7. Long ago, dogs helped people fight wars. Fighters trained the dogs. The dogs learned to bite enemies. The dogs also learned to track enemies who ran away. Explorers who crossed the ocean used these dogs. The dogs could help them when they had to fight in faraway lands.

_____   The story mainly tells

    A. who went across the ocean

    B. how dogs helped people fight

    C. what people did long ago

8. Older Americans have more power today than before. For a long time, older people couldn't work. Everyone thought that they were too old. Older people couldn't get the help they needed. But then they got together. They worked for the things they wanted. They helped each other. And they voted for people who would listen to them.

_____   The story mainly tells

    A. who was too old to get a job

    B. why older Americans have more power

    C. who got together to form clubs

Name_____   Date _____

Read the story. Choose the answer that best completes the sentence.

1. We make sounds by changing the shape of our mouth and throat. Do birds sing this way? Most people did not think so. But scientists have learned that birds sing different notes by changing the shape of their throats. It seems as if they sing like people.

_____ The story mainly tells
   A. how people and birds sing
   B. who uses air to make words
   C. why people like to sing

---

2. Bus companies were getting worried. Fewer and fewer passengers were riding the buses. Then someone had an idea. Airplanes show movies on long trips. Buses on long trips could show movies, too. Some buses now show movies. More people are riding these buses. Today these bus companies have more riders.

_____ The story mainly tells
   A. who takes buses on long trips
   B. how bus companies got more riders
   C. when airplanes show the most movies

---

3. People who fish and people who like turtles are fighting. Some people like to catch fish with nets. But some sea turtles get stuck in the nets and die. Turtle lovers want fishing with nets to be against the law. They want people to fish with a new trap. The trap lets the turtles out but keeps the fish in. People who fish don't like the trap. They say that too many fish get out. They think the trap costs them too much money.

_____ The story mainly tells
   A. why people are fighting over net fishing
   B. which turtles get stuck in the nets
   C. how much the fish traps cost

Comprehension 3, SV 6185-0

Name_____ Date _____

Read the story. Choose the answer that best completes the sentence.

1. There are many colors in the world. All colors are made from a mixture of three colors. These colors are blue, yellow, and red. They are called primary colors. Mix blue and red, and it will make purple. Blue and yellow will give you green. To make orange, mix red and yellow. Black is a mixture of blue, yellow, and red.

_____ The story mainly tells
   A. about the way to make red
   B. how all colors are made from primary colors
   C. which colors to mix to make yellow

2. Ezra Jack Keats wrote the book *The Snowy Day*. He painted all the pictures in it. Keats taught himself to paint. Keats started painting when he was four. As a child he painted on a metal table. He would cover it with pictures. His mother showed them to her friends before cleaning up the table.

_____ The story mainly tells
   A. about Keats's life as a painter
   B. that Keats painted on a board
   C. that Keats didn't have paper for painting

3. Long ago, people used their bodies to measure things. The first finger was used for small things. The width of that finger was a *digit*. A *span* was the width of a hand stretched out. A *cubit* was used to measure larger things. It was the length from the elbow to the tip of the longest finger.

_____ The story mainly tells
   A. how the body was used for measuring things
   B. that a *cubit* measured small things
   C. what was measured with a *digit*

4. A mosaic is a picture that is made from small pieces of stone or glass. The pieces are brightly colored. They are arranged to make a picture. The pieces are pressed into soft plaster. After the plaster hardens, a mosaic is made. Mosaics are used to decorate floors and walls.

_____ The story mainly tells
   A. how fast plaster hardens
   B. what kinds of pictures a mosaic can show
   C. how a mosaic is made

Name _____   Date _____

Read the story. Choose the answer that best completes the sentence.

1. Penguins are birds. But they cannot fly. They use their wings in other ways. They use them for swimming. Their wings are like flippers. In the summer they stay cool by holding their wings away from their bodies. Their wings are put to good use even if they cannot fly.

_____ The story mainly tells
- **A.** where penguins live
- **B.** how penguins use their wings
- **C.** how penguins stay warm

2. The Eiffel Tower is a big tower found in Paris, France. A man named Eiffel designed it for a fair. It is made of steel. It is more than 980 feet high. It weighs more than 7,000 tons. There are 1,652 steps to the top of the tower.

_____ The story mainly tells
- **A.** how big the Eiffel Tower is
- **B.** how many towers there are in France
- **C.** how the Eiffel Tower is used

3. A junk is a kind of boat. Junks sail on the seas of China and Southeast Asia. The sails of a junk have four sides. They are stretched over pieces of wood. Junks are used for fishing. Hong Kong is a very crowded city. So some people even live on their junks. A junk is sometimes a home for more than one family.

_____ The story mainly tells
- **A.** where most people in Hong Kong live
- **B.** about a boat called a junk
- **C.** what junks are made of

4. Emma Lazarus was a poet. She believed that America was the "land of the free." She knew that Jewish people were not treated fairly in many countries. She wanted to help them. So she wrote a poem. It is found on the Statue of Liberty. The statue and her famous poem greet the people who come to America.

_____ The story mainly tells
- **A.** that Lazarus built the Statue of Liberty
- **B.** that Lazarus didn't want to help people
- **C.** that Lazarus wrote about freedom

Name_____   Date _____

Read the story. Choose the answer that best completes the sentence.

1. Many people think sleet and freezing rain are the same thing. But they are not. Sleet is frozen raindrops. Freezing rain is liquid raindrops. Freezing rain does not turn to ice until it hits the ground. Sleet does not stick to trees or wires. But freezing rain does stick to both.

_____ The story mainly tells
- **A.** that sleet sticks to trees and wires
- **B.** that sleet and freezing rain are not the same
- **C.** that freezing rain is more common than sleet

2. When a star dies, a black hole may form. There is strong gravity in a black hole. Anything pulled inside the hole is twisted and stretched. Light is pulled into the hole. But light cannot get out. That is why it's called a black hole.

_____ The story mainly tells
- **A.** about strong gravity
- **B.** how a star dies
- **C.** what a black hole is

3. Porcupines like to eat salty things. A park ranger left his car window down. Sweat from the ranger's hands had coated the steering wheel. Sweat is salty. So what do you think happened? A porcupine ate the steering wheel!

_____ The story mainly tells
- **A.** how a steering wheel got salty
- **B.** why the park ranger left his window open
- **C.** that porcupines eat almost anything salty

4. Stevie Wonder has made music all of his life. When he was 2, he beat a tin pan with a spoon. So his mother bought him a play drum. Then she got him a harmonica. It had a chain. He wore it around his neck. It had 4 holes. So he could play only 4 notes. But Wonder could make music with just 4 notes. He had his first hit record at 12. He even played the harmonica on one of the songs.

_____ The story mainly tells
- **A.** that Wonder has made music all of his life
- **B.** that Wonder made a record when he was 2
- **C.** that Wonder played the drums

Name_____   Date _____

Read the story. Choose the answer that best completes the sentence.

1. The bristlecone pine tree is one of the oldest plants on Earth. Most pine trees live for about 250 years. The bristlecone pine can live more than 4,000 years. It is also one of the slowest growing plants. One tree took 1,500 years to grow 15 feet.

_____ The story mainly tells
     A. where bristlecone pine trees grow
     B. about a kind of old tree that grows slowly
     C. how pine trees don't live long

2. Early settlers made drinks from herbs and weeds. They added yeast to the drinks. The yeast made the drinks fizz. Native Americans also made drinks. But they made drinks from roots and barks. Together the settlers and the Americans made a new drink. They mixed roots and barks with yeast. They invented the first root beer!

_____ The story mainly tells
     A. how root beer was invented
     B. about drinks that the settlers made
     C. that yeast makes drinks fizz

3. The first bus service began in 1662. Blaise Pascal owned the first buses. The buses ran in Paris, France. But his buses were not like buses today. Pascal's buses were pulled by horses. Each bus carried eight riders.

_____ The story mainly tells
     A. that Pascal had only eight buses
     B. about the first bus service
     C. how bus service was slow in 1662

4. A moon is not the same as a planet. A planet is a world that moves around the Sun. A moon is much smaller than a planet. It moves around a planet. All but 2 of our planets have moons. These are Venus and Mercury. Earth and Pluto each have 1 moon. Jupiter has 16 moons!

_____ The story mainly tells
     A. that Earth has two moons
     B. that most planets don't have moons
     C. how a moon and a planet are different

Name_____   Date _____

Read the story. Choose the answer that best completes the sentence.

1. The first person went up into space more than thirty years ago. His name was Yuri Gagarin. He was Russian. His spacecraft was the *Vostok 1*. It circled the earth just one time. Gagarin was in space for less than two hours.

_____   The story mainly tells
     A. about the first manned spaceflight
     B. that *Vostok 1* was a planet
     C. which American was first in space

2. How are a toad and a frog different? A toad spends more time out of water than a frog. Its skin is duller, rougher, and drier. The legs of a toad are shorter, too. A toad cannot jump as far as a frog. A frog lays its eggs in a jelly-like mass. A toad lays its eggs in strings. It wraps the eggs around the stems of water plants.

_____   The story mainly tells
     A. where a frog lays its eggs
     B. how a frog and a toad are different
     C. how far a toad can jump

3. Sitting Bull was a Sioux leader. He didn't want his people to lose their lands. He told the tribes to join against the white settlers. That way they might keep their homeland. In 1876 some tribes camped near the Little Bighorn River. General Custer and his troops charged the group. Sitting Bull's men destroyed the troops. It was a great win for Native Americans.

_____   The story mainly tells
     A. how Custer won the Battle of Little Bighorn
     B. that Sitting Bull was a peaceful man
     C. how Sitting Bull's words helped the Sioux

Name _____   Date _____

Read the story. Choose the answer that best completes the sentence.

1. A geyser is a spring that throws out jets of hot water and steam. One geyser is found in Yellowstone National Park. It is called Old Faithful. It got its name because it spouted once an hour. Since it was found, it has never stopped spouting. It was found in 1870!

_____ The story mainly tells
   A. about the age of Old Faithful
   B. what Yellowstone National Park looks like
   C. about a geyser called Old Faithful

2. One animal has a nose six feet long. That's as big as a tall person! This long-nosed animal is an elephant. An elephant's nose is called a trunk. It lets an elephant breathe and smell. An elephant sucks water with its trunk. Then it gives itself a shower. It also uses its trunk to put food in its mouth.

_____ The story mainly tells
   A. about an animal with a very long nose
   B. why an elephant's nose is called a trunk
   C. how an elephant can give itself a shower

3. The Statue of Liberty is one big woman! Her hand is 16 feet long. One of her fingers is 8 feet long. Her head is 17 feet high. And her eyes are 2 feet wide. Even her fingernails are huge. They are more than 12 inches across.

_____ The story mainly tells
   A. how long some people's fingernails are
   B. how big the Statue of Liberty is
   C. who the tallest woman in the world is

4. Curling began in Scotland. It was played 500 years ago. It is a fun sport. It is played by sweeping ice. Each player has a large stone and a broom. The stones have handles on them. They weigh 35 pounds each. The players slide the stones across the ice toward a target. They sweep the ice in front of the stones to make them travel farther.

_____ The story mainly tells
   A. what a curling stone is made of
   B. how the sport of curling is played
   C. that curling is played in Texas

Name_____   Date _____

Read the story. Choose the answer that best completes the sentence.

1. Did you know that the world's largest bird can't fly? Can you name the bird? It's an ostrich. Why can't it fly? It's too big. An ostrich can be more than 8 feet tall. It can weigh more than 330 pounds. It lives in the grasslands of Africa.

_____   The story mainly tells
- **A.** which zoos have ostriches
- **B.** about the largest bird in the world
- **C.** how well ostriches hunt

2. How fast does the human heart beat? In most people, the heart beats seventy times a minute. A heart rate of fifty beats a minute is normal. But so is a heart rate of one hundred. A healthy heart beats between fifty and one hundred times a minute. A heart beats about three thousand million times in a lifetime!

_____   The story mainly tells
- **A.** about normal heart rates for humans
- **B.** how to measure your heartbeat
- **C.** about the heart rate during a heart attack

3. There are eight notes on a musical scale. Each scale starts and ends with the same letter. One scale is *C, D, E, F, G, A, B, C*. From one *C* to the next *C* is called an octave. An *octave* is the eighth note of a scale. *Octave* comes from the Greek word *okto* meaning "eight."

_____   The story mainly tells
- **A.** what a *C* note is
- **B.** how many scales there are
- **C.** what an octave is

4. Julia Ward Howe wrote many poems and essays. She visited an army camp. She wrote a poem during her stay. It was "The Battle Hymn of the Republic." Later she set her poem to music. She used the tune from "John Brown's Body." "The Battle Hymn of the Republic" became the song of the Union army. It was sung during the Civil War.

_____   The story mainly tells
- **A.** who wrote "John Brown's Body"
- **B.** who won the Civil War
- **C.** about "The Battle Hymn of the Republic"

Name_____   Date _____

Read the story. Choose the answer that best completes the sentence.

1. Jacques Cartier was a French explorer. He made three trips to Canada. Cartier tried to find out what the natives called their land. He asked a few of them. But they didn't understand him. They thought he was asking about their village. So they said, "Kanada." That was their word for *village*. So the huge country of Canada was named after a little village!

_____ The story mainly tells
   A. which countries Cartier explored
   B. how Canada was named after a village
   C. that the natives didn't like Cartier

2. There are many stories about King Arthur. He always met with his knights at a table. It was huge. It seated 150 people. At that time the most important person sat at the head of a table. But King Arthur's table was round. So there wasn't any head of the table. All the seats were equal!

_____ The story mainly tells
   A. how many knights King Arthur had
   B. why King Arthur had a round table
   C. that there are 150 stories about King Arthur

3. Most fish lay eggs. Some fish leave their eggs to hatch by themselves. Other fish watch over their eggs. Mouthbrooders keep their eggs safe. They keep their eggs in their mouths. They even keep their young there. They can eat without swallowing any eggs or young!

_____ The story mainly tells
   A. where most fish lay their eggs
   B. how many eggs a mouthbrooder lays
   C. about the safe place of a mouthbrooder

4. George Herman Ruth liked to play baseball. His nickname was Babe. In 1914 he played for the Boston Red Sox. Ruth was just 19 years old. He played ball for 21 years. Why was he the king of home runs? Because he hit 714 home runs. His record was not broken for 40 years.

_____ The story mainly tells
   A. what a great baseball player Ruth was
   B. that George Ruth changed his name
   C. that Ruth retired in 1935

Name _____   Date _____

Read the story. Choose the answer that best completes the sentence.

1. Peeling an onion can make your eyes water. People try many things to keep from crying. Some people hold an onion under running water. Others try wearing goggles. But goggles make the cook look silly!

_____ The story mainly tells
   A. why onions make people cry
   B. ways to peel an onion without crying
   C. ways to use goggles

2. The thigh bone is the biggest bone in the body. It connects the hip bone to the knee bone. Why does it need to be big and strong? It has to support the weight of the body. It must hold up the leg muscles, too. It needs to be long so that the legs can take wide steps.

_____ The story mainly tells
   A. that the biggest bone is found in the arm
   B. why the thigh bone is so big
   C. how bones help a person walk

3. Have you seen any of Dorothea Lange's pictures? Today many of her works hang in museums. Lange took pictures of poor people. There are pictures of people without jobs. Some pictures show people who lost their homes. Maybe Lange took these pictures because she too had a hard life. Her father went away when she was 12. She never saw him again. Lange was sick for a long time. That left her with a limp for life. Lange had to travel to take pictures. Time away from her children was not easy. Lange died in 1965.

_____ The story mainly tells
   A. about pictures of happy people
   B. that Lange worked in a museum
   C. how Lange's pictures showed people like her

Name _____   Date _____

Read the story. Choose the answer that best completes the sentence.

1. What is the difference between a donkey and a mule? A donkey looks much like a horse. But it has long ears. It has a big head and a short mane. A donkey has two stripes on its back and shoulders. A mule has a horse for a mother and a donkey for a father. A mule is bigger than a donkey. It is stronger, too. But a mule is not as nervous as a donkey.

_____   The story mainly tells
     A. how a donkey and a mule are different
     B. that a donkey has shorter ears than a mule
     C. that donkeys are bigger than mules

---

2. The knife was an early invention. It was used for hunting and carving. In 1699 the King of France made a law about table knives. He ruled that table knives should have round ends. That would stop dinner guests from sticking each other. It would also stop people from picking their teeth with knives. Since then, table knives have had round ends.

_____   The story mainly tells
     A. why table knives have round ends
     B. that people still pick their teeth with knives
     C. that the King of France invented the knife

---

3. When a baby pelican is hungry, it looks for one of its parents. It taps on the parent's bill. The parent opens its mouth. The baby sticks its head inside. Fish that the parent has eaten come up. The baby feeds on this fish. The baby stays in the nest for ten weeks. It will weigh more than its parents. The young bird will live on the extra fat while it learns to catch fish.

_____   The story mainly tells
     A. how pelicans catch fish
     B. about baby pelicans
     C. where pelicans build their nests

Name_____   Date _____

Read the story. Choose the answer that best completes the sentence.

1. Sometimes people can't remember their dreams. But everyone dreams while sleeping. Most people dream two hours every night. In that time they have four or five dreams. Each dream is longer than the dream before. You can tell when someone is dreaming. Their eyeballs move back and forth under their closed eyelids.

_____ The story mainly tells
- **A.** how much sleep people need
- **B.** how often people dream
- **C.** what dreams mean

2. A snake doesn't open its mouth to stick out its tongue. The snake's jaw has a notch that lets the tongue move in and out. The tongue is not poisonous. It is used by the snake to smell. The tongue picks up air and carries it back into the mouth. There are two small holes on the roof of the mouth. It is these holes that smell the air.

_____ The story mainly tells
- **A.** how a snake uses its tongue to smell
- **B.** that a snake's tongue is poisonous
- **C.** that a snake has three holes on its tongue

3. Do you like bananas? Have you ever seen them growing outside? Bananas grow in bunches. A bunch of bananas is called a hand. Bananas grow in big hands. Each banana is called a finger. Each finger grows upward.

_____ The story mainly tells
- **A.** how bananas grow
- **B.** how to eat bananas with your fingers
- **C.** how the banana got its name

4. The fence-painting contest at Tom Sawyer Days is fun. Tom Sawyer is a boy from a well-known book. People dress up like Sawyer for the contest. They run toward a fence they must paint white. They have to paint it very fast. But they must paint it neatly. Most people finish it in about seven seconds!

_____ The story mainly tells
- **A.** how to paint a fence
- **B.** about a fence-painting contest
- **C.** that Tom Sawyer was a painter

Comprehension 3, SV 6185-0

Name_____   Date _____

Read the story. Choose the phrase that best completes the sentence.

1. Many sunken ships lie on the ocean floor. It is hard to raise them. One man found a way. He uses many small balls. Each ball is filled with air so that it floats. He runs a pipe through the inside of the ship. Then he forces the balls through the pipe. Soon the balls fill the ship, and the ship slowly rises.

_____   From this story you can tell
   A. the man was paid well for his idea
   B. the balls are colored blue like the sea
   C. the air in each ball helps raise the ship

2. Most houses are made of wood, nails, and bricks. But a family in California wanted a house that was different. So they built their house with foam. They laid big sheets of plastic on the ground. Then they used fans to blow air under the sheets. When the sheets looked like large balloons, the family covered the sheets with foam. After the foam dried, they painted it the color of rocks.

_____   From this story you can tell
   A. the house looked like a rocky hill
   B. the house was painted blue and white
   C. part of the house was made of bricks

3. The first year of life is very important for babies. During this time they eat their first food. They take their first steps. They say their first words. Babies also grow very fast. They gain about two pounds a month. They also grow ten inches taller. If a child grew this fast every year, a ten-year-old child would be ten feet tall!

_____   From this story you can tell
   A. older children grow slower than babies
   B. people stop learning things after age ten
   C. some ten-year-olds are very, very tall

Go on to the next page.

Name_____   **Date** _____

4. Some hotels have very fancy rooms. One hotel has a room that looks like a cave. It has rock walls. There's even a waterfall in the bathroom. The fireplace looks like the door to a cave. When you lie down in the bed, you can look up at the rocks. Why did the hotel owners take the trouble to build such a room? Many of their plain rooms are often empty. But the cave room has people staying in it almost all the time.

_____ From this story you can tell
   A. the people like the cave room better than a plain room
   B. the cave room costs fifty dollars a night
   C. the cave room is often empty

5. There is a man who makes music by playing water glasses. He buys plain glasses at the store. Then he puts them on a table and fills them with water. He fills some glasses full. He fills others halfway. He pours just a little water in the rest of the glasses. Then he plays by running his wet finger around the tops of the glasses. He changes the sounds by adding water or pouring water out of the glasses.

_____ From this story you can tell
   A. this man really likes to play the harp
   B. the amount of water changes the sound
   C. the man uses 15 glasses to play a song

6. The peanut plant is a strange plant. Peanuts are like nuts, but nuts grow on trees. Peanuts grow on bushy plants. They begin to grow on the plant's stem. Then the stem turns and grows down toward the ground. It pushes into the soft earth. It keeps growing farther and farther down. To see if the peanuts are ready to pick, the farmer has to dig them up!

_____ From this story you can tell
   A. peanut plants are like trees
   B. peanuts are ready to pick in the fall
   C. peanuts grow under the ground

Comprehension 3, SV 6185-0

Name_____   Date _____

Read the story. Choose the phrase that best completes the sentence.

1.   Barney stepped back to look at his work. He leaned his head to one side as he gazed at the canvas. Then he wiped his hands with a rag and cleaned all his brushes.

_____ From this story you can tell
   A.   Barney is a painter
   B.   Barney is a cook
   C.   Barney is a dentist

2.   The phone rang. Mrs. Bond answered it and talked for some time to the caller. As she spoke she played nervously with her hair. At one point she covered her eyes with her hand. When she got off the phone, Mrs. Bond sighed and went to the window. She stood there for a while, staring out but seeing nothing.

_____ From this story you can tell
   A.   that the call was good news
   B.   that the call caused her to worry
   C.   that the call was from a friendly neighbor

3.   Mack awoke with a start and jumped out of bed. He realized that he had slept through the alarm again. Quickly he threw on his clothes and hunted for his socks and shoes. Minutes later Mack was flying down the street to the bus stop. At the bus stop, his feet felt funny. Something was wrong. When Mack looked down and saw what he had done, he shook his head and laughed.

_____ From this story you can tell
   A.   Mack's socks were different colors
   B.   Mack's shoes were on the wrong feet
   C.   Mack forgot his coat

4.   A hungry wolf met a fat, well-fed dog. "Come home with me!" said the dog. "My master will feed you every day. All you have to do is wear a collar and follow orders." The wolf said, "Thanks anyway. I would rather go hungry but be free than be well fed and a slave."

_____ From this story you can tell
   A.   the wolf did not need food
   B.   the owner was unkind to the dog
   C.   the wolf did not go home with the dog

Name_____   Date _____

Read the story. Choose the phrase that best completes the sentence.

1. Without bees, some of our prettiest flowers would never bloom. Flowers make a special dust. A bee flies to different flowers and drinks the flower's sweet juice. As the bee drinks, it is covered with this dust. It carries the dust with it. At the next flower, the bee drinks again. The dust falls on the flower's seeds. This helps the flower seeds grow. Then these plants become flowers.

_____   From this story you can tell
    A. the flowers and the bees need each other
    B. bees are bad for most kinds of plants
    C. bees do not like the dust that gets on them

2. There were many factories in the city. The factories turned the air black with smoke. One morning there was a heavy fog. People began to have trouble breathing. Many people called their doctor or went to the hospital. Finally it rained, and the fog lifted. The people began to feel better. Without the fog they could breathe easily again.

_____   From this story you can tell
    A. the doctors didn't have very much work
    B. the people got sick from the smoke and fog
    C. the rain sent many people to the hospital

3. At one time a cat that caught mice cost four days' pay. If you killed a cat, you had to give its owner a sheep and a lamb. Or you could pay with a pile of grain. To measure the grain, someone held the dead cat by its tail. Its nose touched the ground. Grain was poured out until the cat was covered. This pile of grain paid for the food that mice ate because the cat was not around.

_____   From this story you can tell
    A. a dead cat was worth more than a live one
    B. kittens were better to have than cats
    C. cats cost so much because they ate mice

Name_____   Date _____

Read the story. Choose the phrase that best completes the sentence.

1. The homeless children were often tired and sick. Their skin was red. The doctor wondered why the children were this way. The doctor thought about the food he ate. He ate meat and drank milk. He almost never got sick. He thought about the food that poor children ate. It wasn't very healthy food. So the doctor decided to feed meat and milk to the sick children. The children got better very soon.

_____   From this story you can tell
- **A.** eating well helps people stay healthy
- **B.** only children get sick
- **C.** drinking milk makes people's skin red

2. A company makes a machine that helps babies sleep. People can put the machine on their baby's bed. The machine shakes the bed softly. The shaking feels just like a ride in a car. The machine also makes noise. But this noise sounds like the wind blowing against a car window.

_____   From this story you can tell
- **A.** babies like the sound of the ocean
- **B.** babies don't like the machine very much
- **C.** many babies sleep when they ride in cars

3. "My garden! My corn!" Ellie cried. The garden looked awful. Most of the corn plants were broken. Many ears of corn had been eaten. Some of the young plants lay on the ground. Ellie looked at the ground that was still wet. It had rained two days before. Then she spotted some tracks about two inches long. The tracks led from the garden to the woods.

_____   From this story you can tell
- **A.** this was Ellie's first garden
- **B.** the wind and rain broke the corn plants
- **C.** there had been an animal in the garden

Name_____   Date _____

Read the story. Choose the phrase that best completes the sentence.

1. Fred Gipson was a famous writer. As a boy he loved stories. Fred's grandfather told him many stories. Once Fred's grandfather told him about a big, yellow dog. This dog saved a man from a sick wolf. Later Fred wrote a book about this dog. The title of his book was *Old Yeller*.

_____   From this story you can tell
    A. Fred's book was about a yellow wolf
    B. Fred used a story to write a book
    C. Fred's book was about his grandfather

2. Today most people eat with a knife, fork, and spoon. But people didn't always use these things. The knife is the oldest of the three. The first knives were made of stone. People have used some kind of knife for more than a million years. The first spoons were just scooped-out pieces of wood. People have used spoons for twenty thousand years. The fork came into use only five hundred years ago.

_____   From this story you can tell
    A. people have used forks longer than spoons
    B. people have used spoons longer than forks
    C. people have always used forks

3. The longest cave in the world is Mammoth Cave. It is found in Flint Ridge, Kentucky. This cave runs under the ground for more than two hundred miles. The cave is full of strange things. There are many tall, limestone columns. There are lakes and even a river inside the cave. This river is called the Echo River. It runs almost four hundred feet under the ground.

_____   From this story you can tell
    A. Mammoth Cave is above the ground
    B. it is fun to sail on the Echo River
    C. a trip through the cave would take time

Name _____   Date _____

Read the story. Choose the phrase that best completes the sentence.

1. Have you ever looked at a map of the United States? Many states have strange shapes. The bottom part of Michigan looks like a mitten. Maine looks like the head of a buffalo. Tennessee is shaped like a sled. Also, California looks like an arm. Try to remember these strange shapes. They will help you remember the states.

_____ From this story you can tell
  A. many states have different shapes
  B. Maine has the shape of a mitten
  C. the shapes will help you forget the states

2. In Europe most people eat with the fork held in the left hand. Most Americans hold it in their right hand. Why is it different? In the pioneer days, there was not always enough food to eat. So people ate very fast. They could eat even faster by holding the fork in their right hand.

_____ From this story you can tell
  A. pioneers liked to eat slowly
  B. everyone holds the fork in their left hand
  C. Americans and Europeans eat differently

3. The Germans had a special idea for birthday parties. The birthday cake always had candles on it. They would always put one more candle than the age of the child. So if the child was five, the cake had six candles. The extra candle stood for the "light of life." It was a wish for good health in the coming year.

_____ From this story you can tell
  A. the extra candle had a special meaning
  B. the cake had more candles than frosting
  C. the Germans did not like birthdays

Name_____   Date _____

Read the story. Choose the phrase that best completes the sentence.

1. Today you can find buttons on many clothes. But buttons have not always been used to fasten clothes. Only belts and pins were used before to join parts of clothes. For hundreds of years, buttons were used like jewels. They were put on clothes just for their beauty. Finally in the 1200s, buttons were used as fasteners on clothes.

_____ From this story you can tell
    A. buttons are still used only for beauty
    B. pins and belts are better than buttons
    C. buttons joined belts and pins as fasteners

2. Marco Polo was a famous traveler. His home was in Venice, Italy. In 1271 he made a trip to the Far East. In China he became friends with the ruler. His name was Kublai Khan. Polo became his helper. He stayed in China for twenty years. Then he went back home. There he wrote a book. The book told all about the Far East.

_____ From this story you can tell
    A. Polo got lost on his trip
    B. Venice is west of China
    C. Polo did not stay long in China

3. Have you ever seen someone turn a thumbs up? Today a thumbs up means good luck. The early Egyptians used a thumbs up to mean hope. They also used it to mean winning. To them a thumbs down meant losing or bad luck. For the early Romans, a thumbs up meant life. A thumbs down meant death.

_____ From this story you can tell
    A. a thumbs up means bad luck
    B. the early Romans did not have thumbs
    C. a thumbs up means good things

Name_____   Date _____

Read the story. Choose the phrase that best completes the sentence.

1. Times change and so do prices. In the 1930s you could go to the movies for ten cents. For that price you saw a movie and a cartoon! At that time one of the big movie stars was a little girl. Her name was Shirley Temple.

_____   From this story you can tell
    A. Shirley Temple is still a little girl
    B. some things cost less in the 1930s
    C. Temple's picture is found on a dime

2. Jeanne d'Arc was a famous French girl. She lived more than five hundred years ago. At that time France was at war with England. D'Arc began hearing voices in her head. The voices told her to help her country. So she became the leader of the French army. Together they beat the English army. Most of the French people loved her for this. But some people did not like d'Arc. They thought she was a witch because of the voices she heard. At age 19 d'Arc was burned at the stake.

_____   From this story you can tell
    A. d'Arc lived in England
    B. all the people loved d'Arc
    C. d'Arc did what the voices told her to do

3. The albatross is a big bird. It lives near the sea. This bird can sometimes fly for six days without moving its wings. The albatross knows how to glide on air streams. It has more wing feathers than other birds. This bird can even sleep while flying!

_____   From this story you can tell
    A. the albatross has a hidden motor
    B. the albatross can fly very well
    C. the albatross is a lazy bird

Name_____   Date _____

Read the story. Choose the phrase that best completes the sentence.

1. Some towns in the United States have strange names. Many of these names are not English. Take Baton Rouge as an example. It's the capital of Louisiana. Its name comes from French words. *Baton rouge* means "red stick." Long ago, Native Americans used red sticks to mark off their hunting grounds. The French settlers named the town after these red sticks.

_____   From this story you can tell
    A. the names of towns are not always English
    B. Baton Rouge is a French settler's name
    C. Louisiana is part of England

2. There are different ways to tell how hot or cold it is outside. But do you know a fun way to measure the heat? First you must listen for the cricket chirps. Then you need to count the chirps for 15 seconds. Then add 40 to the number of chirps. Your answer should be close to the real temperature.

_____   From this story you can tell
    A. crickets chirp louder when it is cold
    B. only crickets are used to measure the heat
    C. crickets chirp faster as the heat rises

3. Charles Blondin was a brave man. In 1859 he crossed Niagara Falls on a tightrope. Then he put on a blindfold and crossed the rushing water again. But that wasn't all he did. He walked the rope with stilts. As his last trick, he walked halfway across the tightrope. There he stopped for breakfast! He cooked some eggs and ate them. Then he made his way to the other side.

_____   From this story you can tell
    A. Blondin was a poor swimmer
    B. Blondin was comfortable on the tightrope
    C. Blondin was not afraid of water

Name _____   Date _____

Read the story. Choose the phrase that best completes the sentence.

1. Big Bend is a very large park. It is found in West Texas. The park covers thousands of square miles. The park is full of mountains and canyons. The land is rough and rocky. There is a story that tells why Big Bend is this way. It goes back to when the earth was being made. The story says that the extra parts were dropped into Big Bend.

_____   From this story you can tell
  A. Big Bend is a clock
  B. the park is found in West Virginia
  C. why Big Bend is so rocky

2. Whooping cough makes people very sick. Today it is cured with medicine. But four hundred years ago, people got rid of it in other ways. One way was to put a live frog in the sick person's mouth. Another way was to hold a spider near the sick person's head. Then the cough was told to go away.

_____   From this story you can tell
  A. ways to treat whooping cough have changed
  B. frogs are a good cure for many things
  C. a frog a day keeps the doctor away

3. April 22 is known as Earth Day. On this day people honor our planet, Earth. Earth is our home. We must remember to take care of it. Earth Day is a good time for picking up litter. Cleaning a park is a good idea. But we should help our Earth every day.

_____   From this story you can tell
  A. Earth Day takes place in August
  B. Earth sometimes needs help
  C. we should not help clean up litter

Name_____   Date _____

Read the story. Choose the phrase that best completes the sentence.

1. Tom Thumb was a famous circus star. His real name was Charles Stratton. As a grown-up, Thumb was just forty inches tall. In his circus act, Thumb had fights for fun with tall people. He sang, danced, and joked, too. Thumb had fans all over the world. He even met the Queen of England and Abraham Lincoln. Thumb did not let his small size trouble him. He once said, "I feel I am as big as anybody."

_____   From this story you can tell
    A. Thumb's small size made him famous
    B. Abraham Lincoln acted in a circus
    C. Thumb was no bigger than a thumb

2. Some of the names of American states are French. For example, *Vermont* means "green mountain." Maine was named after a place in France. Louisiana was named after a French king.

_____   From this story you can tell
    A. Maine was named after a king
    B. some states do not have English names
    C. Louisiana is the name of a mountain

3. Baseball is a fun game. Today many people play it. But long ago it was played in a different way. In the 1830s baseball was called town ball. Big rocks were used as bases. The playing field was square. The pitcher was known as the feeder. The batter was called the striker. When the batter hit the ball, he ran clockwise around the bases. A fielder would throw the ball at the runner. If the ball hit the runner, he was out!

_____   From this story you can tell
    A. baseball was once called football
    B. town ball used a round field
    C. some baseball rules have changed

Name _____   Date _____

Read the story. Choose the phrase that best completes the sentence.

1. Angel Falls is a waterfall in Venezuela. Venezuela is a country in South America. Angel Falls is the highest waterfall in the world. It is a part of the Churún River. Its waters drop more than half a mile. Angel Falls was named after an American. His name was Jim Angel. He found the waterfall while hunting for gold.

_____ From this story you can tell
    A. the Churún River is not very deep
    B. Angel Falls is found on a mountain
    C. Jim Angel found a gold mine

---

2. Do you like peanuts? Many people do. In fact, March is known as Peanut Month. People in the United States eat many peanuts. They eat more than one billion pounds of peanuts a year. Half of this is eaten as peanut butter.

_____ From this story you can tell
    A. peanuts are a favorite American snack
    B. May is Peanut Month
    C. peanut butter is made from walnuts

---

3. The year was 1960. Chubby Checker was only 19 years old. Checker liked to dance. But he was tired of the same old dances. He wanted a new dance. So he made up a few new steps. The dance was called the Twist. He even wrote a song to go along with his new dance. Soon young people everywhere were doing the Twist.

_____ From this story you can tell
    A. people did not like Checker's new song
    B. Checker never learned to dance
    C. the Twist became a well-known dance

Name _____   Date _____

Read the story. Choose the phrase that best completes the sentence.

1. Do you like pigs? Some people do. In fact, some people keep pigs as pets. Pigs are not really dirty animals. They really don't even smell bad. But they do like to roll around in the mud. This helps them keep cool. Did you know that pigs even have their own day? It's March 1, and it's called National Pig Day.

_____ From this story you can tell
  A. pigs hate mud
  B. National Pig Day is in April
  C. pigs can make good pets

2. People once had to buy most of their food fresh. There were no frozen foods. Some foods were treated with salt to make them last longer. Vinegar was used to treat foods, too. Then in the 1920s, a man had an idea. His name was Charles Birdseye. His idea was to quick-freeze foods. His new idea was a success.

_____ From this story you can tell
  A. salt freezes foods
  B. quick-freezing is a good way to store foods
  C. vinegar made foods taste better

3. Every year people invent strange things. Sometimes these things are of some use. Many times they are not. Eyeglasses for chickens are an example. Chickens like to peck at each other. So someone made a pair of eyeglasses for chickens to wear. They were strapped on the birds' heads. They were meant to protect the chickens' eyes!

_____ From this story you can tell
  A. the eyeglasses for chickens were of no use
  B. the eyeglasses helped the chickens read
  C. all chickens wear glasses today

Name_____   Date _____

Read the story. Choose the sentence that best answers the question.

1. One orange is left in the bowl. You touch and smell it. The orange feels soft and mushy. It has a sharp smell. Part of the skin is broken. There is something white and powdery on the skin. You decide not to eat the orange.

_____ Which of these sentences is probably true?
  A. Eating the orange may make you sick.
  B. The orange is not ripe yet.
  C. The orange should be used for juice.

---

2. The Brooklyn Bridge links Brooklyn and Manhattan in New York. It is very long. The bridge hangs from long steel cables that are 16 inches thick. Two huge towers hold up the cables. The bridge has six lanes for cars and trucks.

_____ Which of these statements is probably true?
  A. The bridge can hold many cars and trucks.
  B. The Brooklyn Bridge is the world's largest bridge.
  C. The bridge is never used by people.

---

3. American settlers had a hard time moving west. They had to travel over mountains and through thick forests. For years they followed small trails made by Native Americans. In 1811 the government made one of the trails into a road. People could then go all the way from Maryland to Illinois. You can still travel from Washington, D.C., to St. Louis, Missouri, on this road.

_____ Which of these sentences is probably true?

  A. Some roads were once small trails.
  B. Roads are hard to build.
  C. Native Americans helped build the road.

---

4. Terns are sea birds that are like gulls. A tern is about 15 inches long. It is a strong flier. One kind of tern flies from the North Pole to the South Pole and back each year. Terns eat fish. They build nests near coasts.

_____ Which of these sentences is probably true?
  A. Terns live near the middle of the earth.
  B. Terns can fly long distances.
  C. Terns lay three eggs each year.

Go on to the next page.

Name_____   Date _____

5. "Leave the hall light on, please," Luis called. "And please don't close the door." Luis's mom and dad had gone out. Tía Rosa was putting Luis to bed.

_____   Which of these sentences is probably true?
   A. Luis is afraid of the dark.
   B. Luis's mom and dad will be back in a week.
   C. It is time for Luis to eat.

6. The Constitution has all the laws of the United States. It tells what people can and cannot do. It tells what states can and cannot do. The Constitution also tells about the duties of the president. It tells how people can pass new laws. It tells whose job it is to see that the laws are followed.

_____   Which of these sentences is probably true?
   A. The Constitution affects people in the United States.
   B. The President writes the Constitution.
   C. The Constitution cannot be changed.

7. A lake is a body of water. Lakes are surrounded on all sides by land. A gulf is a body of water that is not surrounded by land on all sides. A gulf opens into an ocean. Because of this a gulf is much like an ocean. Gulfs can be deep. Ocean fish live in gulfs. So do ocean shellfish. Two big gulfs touch North America.

_____   Which of these sentences is probably true?
   A. Ocean plants can live in a gulf.
   B. Gulfs are sometimes lakes.
   C. Fishing isn't safe in a gulf.

8. He told people in America how to live and work. They didn't like the king. He made them pay a tax for a war they did not fight. The Americans did not want to pay the tax.

_____   Which of these sentences is probably true?
   A. Americans gladly helped the English king.
   B. Americans thought that the tax was unfair.
   C. Americans still have a king.

Name_____   Date _____

Read the story. Choose the sentence that best answers the question.

1.   Holland is a country that is next to the sea. Dikes, or walls, are built
around the towns in Holland. The walls keep the sea from flooding the towns.
One day a boy saw a small hole in the dike near his town. Sea water was
running out of the hole. And the hole was getting bigger. He put his finger in
the hole and called for help. He waited a long time. Finally some people came
to help. At last the boy could go home. He knew that the town was safe.

_____   Which of these sentences is probably true?
   A. The people fixed the hole.
   B. The boy fixed the hole by himself.
   C. The people thought the boy was silly.

---

2.   Shree walked to the ticket counter. She waited in line. Five other people
were buying tickets. She heard people asking for seats. Some talked about left
field. Others said, "One near first base." One person said, "Behind home plate."

_____   Which of these sentences is probably true?
   A. Shree was going on a train trip.
   B. Shree was buying a ticket to the
         baseball game.
   C. Shree was in line at the movie theater.

---

3.   Train tracks have signals to keep the trains from hitting each other. The
train track is divided into blocks. Electricity flows through each block of track.
When a train moves along the track, it runs over a switch. The switch turns on
a red light. A train coming from another direction sees the red light. It stops so
the two trains will not crash into each other.

_____   Which of these sentences is probably true?
   A. Trains obey the signals.
   B. Red lights always mean "go."
   C. Trains always go the same way.

Name_____   Date _____

Read the story. Choose the sentence that best answers the question.

1.   Kim gets up and goes out for the paper every morning. Then she eats breakfast and reads the comics with her mom. One day the paper stopped coming. It did not come for a week. Kim and her mom wondered what was wrong. Then Kim's mom found an envelope that was addressed to the paper. She had forgotten to mail it.

_____   Which of these sentences is probably true?
  A. Kim's mom had not paid the bill for the paper.
  B. A new person was delivering the paper.
  C. Kim's mom had paid for the paper.

2.   A drug is something that causes a change in the body. Medicines are drugs that can help parts of the body work better. Medicines can make people feel better when they are sick. But some kinds of drugs can hurt the body. Some drugs make the heart work too fast or too slow. Some drugs make people act in ways that are not safe. Certain drugs can cause death.

_____   Which of these sentences is probably true?
  A. People should never use medicines.
  B. Medicines should be used with care.
  C. All medicines make people sick.

3.   Bill got on his bike. He rode down the street past homes and trees. Then he reached the park. There he put on his shin pads and his cleats. He began kicking the round ball back and forth between his feet.

_____   Which of these sentences is probably true?
  A. Bill went to play soccer.
  B. Bill went to his job after school.
  C. Bill was on an errand for his grandmother.

Name_____   Date _____

Read the story. Choose the sentence that best answers the question.

1.   Juan worked after school at a small shop. He made deliveries for the owner. One day the owner told Juan to make a delivery. Juan looked at the box. It had his address on it. Juan asked, "Is this right?" The owner told Juan to take the box to that address. When Juan got to the address, all his friends were there. They sang "Happy Birthday" to Juan.

_____   Which of these sentences is probably true?
   A. The owner wanted to celebrate Juan's birthday.
   B. Juan didn't get along well with the owner.
   C. Juan got the job through a class at school.

2.   Cars use gasoline for fuel. When the fuel burns, a harmful gas goes into the air. The gas is carbon dioxide. A car gives off other harmful gases, too. These gases make the air all over the earth dirty. In some places it is not safe for some people to breathe. Dirty air hurts their lungs. It can cause heart problems.

_____   Which of these sentences is probably true?
   A. Cars can make the air dirty.
   B. Dirty air is good for your lungs.
   C. Cars help clean the air.

3.   Jim Thorpe was a star athlete. Playing sports was easy for him. He played baseball and football. He also won medals for running track at the Olympic games.

_____   Which of these sentences is probably true?
   A. Track is harder than baseball.
   B. Baseball was Thorpe's best sport.
   C. Thorpe could play more than one sport.

4.   Bill and his dad got into the car. They were going to the store. They backed out of the driveway. Both of them heard a noise in the back of the car. As they drove, the noise got louder. The car bumped up and down. They pulled over and stopped the car. When they stepped out of the car, they noticed that it sagged to one side.

_____   Which of these sentences is probably true?
   A. Bill and his dad rode on a motorcycle.
   B. The car was wet.
   C. The car had a flat tire.

Name_____   Date _____

Read the story. Choose the sentence that best answers the question.

1. Brown Bear was a Delaware Indian. He learned to hunt from his father. Brown Bear and his father hunted for food. His mother and sister followed them. They were gone for many days. After the hunt the family fixed the meat of the animals they killed. They made clothes and tents from the skins of the animals. They made tools from the bones and other parts.

_____   Which of these sentences is probably true?
  A. The Delaware lived only on fish.
  B. Brown Bear taught himself to hunt.
  C. A Delaware Indian family worked together.

---

2. Have you heard traffic news today? It may have come from a person in a helicopter high above the city. A helicopter has blades on the top of it. It does not have wings. The blades spin fast. Then air rushes up and over the blades. The moving air pushes the helicopter straight up. When it's time to land, the helicopter can come straight down.

_____   Which of these sentences is probably true?
  A. Helicopters don't fly very well.
  B. Few people ever ride in helicopters.
  C. Helicopters can land and take off in small spaces.

---

3. Look around. Do you see something made of bricks? People have built things with bricks for thousands of years. Old bricks have been found all over the world. Most bricks are made of clay. The clay is mixed with water to make a stiff mud. Then the bricks are shaped and baked. Today bricks are used to build houses. In the past, bricks were also used to make streets.

_____   Which of these sentences is probably true?
  A. People do not use bricks anymore.
  B. Early Americans built many things with bricks they made.
  C. Bricks were first used on streets.

Name_____   Date _____

Read the story. Choose the sentence that best answers the question.

1. May was on the road. She saw a plane over her car. It was a warm day, and the windows were rolled down. May heard the plane's engine go off and then on. This happened many times. The plane turned and came in low over the road. The plane turned again. May pulled off the road.

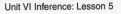

_____ Which of these sentences is probably true?
   A. May was waiting for her mother.
   B. The plane had problems and needed to land.
   C. The pilot was counting the cars on the road.

2. When a ship goes from New York City to Cape Town, South Africa, it must cross the line that divides the earth. This line is called the equator. It divides north and south. When the ship crosses this line, people on the ship have a party. Everyone who is crossing this line for the first time must do tricks. When they all have had a turn, the party ends.

_____ Which of these sentences is probably true?
   A. The equator is a row of cans in the ocean.
   B. A ship cannot go from New York to Cape Town.
   C. The equator is an important line.

3. The Tennessee River runs through high hills. For years the river flooded. Water ran over the banks of the river. The water ruined fields and houses. People built a high dam. Water collected behind the dam. This made a lake. When it rained, the floodwater went into the lake.

_____ Which of these sentences is probably true?
   A. The Tennessee River dried up.
   B. Dams help stop flooding.
   C. River water is not safe to drink.

Name _____   Date _____

Read the story. Choose the sentence that best answers the question.

1. All birds do not have the same kind of beaks. Some birds have short, strong beaks. These birds eat seeds. They can crack open the seeds and eat them. Some birds eat insects. These birds must have beaks that help them get to insects in the ground and inside tree trunks.

_____   Which of these sentences is probably true?

A. Birds need people to help them when they eat.

B. Birds that eat insects need long, pointed beaks.

C. Birds do not make good pets.

2. Thousands of people lived in New Orleans in 1830. All around the town were swamps. Mosquitoes lived in the swamps. People began to get sick and die. They died from a disease called yellow fever. More and more people died. It took a long time for doctors to learn that the mosquitoes gave people yellow fever.

_____   Which of these sentences is probably true?

A. Yellow fever was hard to cure.

B. Only children got yellow fever.

C. Doctors didn't get yellow fever.

3. Jazz is a kind of music. People first played jazz in America. When people play jazz, they make up the songs as they play. This makes jazz seem new all the time.

_____   Which of these sentences is probably true?

A. Jazz music is always changing.

B. No one plays jazz today.

C. Jazz music always stays the same.

4. First you need to make the ground ready. Break up the big pieces of dirt with a hoe. Use a shovel to take out all the rocks. Make sure there are no weeds or grass in the dirt. Then make straight lines in the dirt. Poke little holes in the lines. Keep the holes about one inch apart. Next put seeds in the holes.

_____   Which of these sentences is probably true?

A. This is one way to rake leaves.

B. This tells how to make a path.

C. This is a good way to make a garden.

Comprehension 3, SV 6185-0

Name _____   Date _____

Read the story. Choose the sentence that best answers the question.

1. Oil is a resource. So are coal and gas. They are fuels. We burn these fuels to make heat and power. We use gas and oil to run our cars. All three of these resources come from the earth. They were formed long before people lived on the earth.

_____ Which of these sentences is probably true?
  A. No one uses resources.
  B. Oil, gas, and coal are not resources.
  C. Oil, coal, and gas help people to meet needs.

2. In the 1800s a man from France wanted people all over the world to know that America stood for freedom. He asked an artist friend to help him. First the artist drew a picture of a woman wearing a long robe. He showed the woman holding a torch and wearing a crown. The statue was finished in 1885. Now it stands on Liberty Island. It has greeted many people who have come to America.

_____ Which of these sentences is probably true?
  A. The man's statue was never finished.
  B. The statue is The Statue of Liberty.
  C. The statue stands for all artists.

3. Even though she didn't speak, I knew Mom was mad. Her face was red. Her hands were on her hips. She was standing in the door, tapping her foot. I was late again. I tried to run up to my room fast.

_____ Which of these sentences is probably true?
  A. Mom was pleased with me.
  B. People can say things without using words.
  C. Mom shouted, and I knew she was mad.

4. The two children lay on their backs in the grass. They were looking up at the sky. "I see a whale. See him spout!" said one. "That doesn't look like a whale," said the other. "It looks like an elephant." Neither could agree on the shapes they saw.

_____ Which of these sentences is probably true?
  A. The children were watching cartoons outside.
  B. An elephant was riding a whale.
  C. The children were seeing shapes in the clouds.

Name_____   Date _____

Read the story. Choose the sentence that best answers the question.

1. How is the air heated in a hot-air balloon? Pilots use a gas flame to heat the air. If a pilot wants to go up, he or she shoots the flame up into the balloon. This makes the air hot. The pilot must cool the air to go down. Once the balloon is up, the wind guides the balloon. If there is no wind, the balloon stays in one place.

_____   Which of these sentences is probably true?
   A. Hot air makes the balloon rise.
   B. Balloons get you places fast.
   C. Hot-air balloons fly with wings.

2. Some insects have built-in ways to hide from their enemies. One insect looks just like a stick. Its body is long, thin, and brown. Its legs are very thin. When birds see it, they think it is a twig. So they don't eat it. Another insect looks like a leaf. It is green and flat, and it hangs on a plant. Birds think it is part of the plant.

_____   Which of these sentences is probably true?
   A. Birds are not very smart.
   B. Some insects are shaped like parts of plants.
   C. Insects love to play tricks.

3. We put all the books away in boxes. The teacher took our little bits of crayon and threw them away. She put our big ones in a box. Some children took the pictures off the walls. I washed the chalkboard. The janitor came in to lock the windows. The teacher put her plants in a box to take home.

_____   Which of these sentences is probably true?
   A. It is the first day of school.
   B. It is the last day of school.
   C. There has been a fire at school.

Name _____   Date _____

Read the story. Choose the sentence that best answers the question.

1. Long ago, life was hard for the settlers who lived on the prairie. Often they lived far away from other people. So there wasn't much help if there was trouble. They had to make homes out of dirt because there weren't many trees. And there were always wild animals that roamed the prairie. The settlers had to raise all their own food. But sometimes it didn't rain for months, and all their crops died.

_____ Which of these sentences is probably true?
- **A.** The settlers were brave people.
- **B.** The prairie was always wet and muddy.
- **C.** The settlers shopped for food in the East.

2. Jack looked up. He saw the same thing he had seen each day this week. The geese were flying south. He heard them honking as they went. "Too bad," he thought. "It will soon be cold and snowy. I'll have to play inside."

_____ Which of these sentences is probably true?
- **A.** The geese spoke with Jack about the weather.
- **B.** Flying geese can mean a change of season.
- **C.** Jack works in a birdhouse.

3. Maria did not look up when the teacher spoke. She did not hear what she was supposed to do with the paper. She walked to the teacher's desk to ask. She watched the teacher's lips as he spoke. When the teacher turned his head and spoke, Maria did not hear what he said.

_____ Which of these sentences is probably true?
- **A.** Maria needs to be a better listener.
- **B.** Maria cannot see the paper.
- **C.** Maria reads lips to understand people.

4. There are several ways to help a forest that is quickly losing its trees. One way is to plant young trees, or seedlings. These trees replace those that die or are cut down. And they grow quickly. Sometimes people fly over a forest and drop seeds. New trees will sprout from these seeds.

_____ Which of these sentences is probably true?
- **A.** It is important to keep forests from dying.
- **B.** Trees never die in a forest.
- **C.** People don't really care about forests.

Name _____   Date _____

Read the story. Choose the sentence that best answers the question.

1.   Kate counted out five pairs of socks. She put one extra pair in the pile. She found the T-shirt she liked to sleep in. She chose some shorts and shirts. "Don't forget your teddy bear," her dad called.

_____   Which of these sentences is probably true?
   A.   Kate wants to see how many socks she has.
   B.   Kate doesn't like nightgowns.
   C.   Kate is getting ready for a trip.

2.   Your skin is made of a thick layer of tiny, living parts called cells. Your skin helps keep you alive. It holds in the moisture that your body must have. Sometimes skin from one part of the body can be put onto another part. This is called a skin graft. Skin grafts can help someone who has had a bad burn.

_____   Which of these sentences is probably true?
   A.   Skin grafts don't work.
   B.   Skin grows on only one part of the body.
   C.   A skin graft can save a person's life.

3.   A cave is a hole under the ground. Most caves are formed in rock called limestone. Caves are made by water. Water eats away part of the rock. Over many years a small hole or crack in a rock becomes very big. Then it becomes a home for bears or bats. And it becomes a place people want to explore.

_____   Which of these sentences is probably true?
   A.   Water collects in limestone cracks.
   B.   Animals stay away from caves.
   C.   Caves are open to the sun.

4.   Could you buy a candy bar today with a seashell? No. But long ago, people used seashells as money. In Africa, you could buy a goat for one hundred seashells. You can still find these shells on the beach. They are about the size of a bean. But don't try to buy a candy bar with them. They're not worth a penny.

_____   Which of these sentences is probably true?
   A.   Long ago it was good to have many seashells.
   B.   Today people shop with seashells.
   C.   Wood is made from seashells.

Name _____   Date _____

Read the story. Choose the sentence that best answers the question.

1.   Eskimo sculpture is beautiful. People come from all around to buy it. They like the simple animal shapes that the Eskimos carve out of soapstone or animal bones. Eskimos carve the shapes of the animals that live around them.

_____   Which of these sentences is probably true?
   A. The Eskimos make art from nature.
   B. You can wash with soapstone.
   C. Eskimos are not good artists.

2.   The spring was very wet. A pond formed in the field. Children playing in the field saw a duck swimming in the pond. Soon it warmed up, and the pond dried up. The duck came back to the pond with some baby ducks. But there was no water. The children brought out a plastic swimming pool. They filled the pool with water. The mother duck jumped in, but the babies could not.

_____   Which of these sentences is probably true?
   A. The babies couldn't jump over the side of the pool.
   B. The mother duck didn't want the babies to swim.
   C. Many people don't like ducks.

3.   Frank rode his horse as fast as he could. He swung his lasso above his head. The cows were running all around him. It was very dusty. Frank's dad was standing at the fence. The gate to the corral was open.

_____   Which of these sentences is probably true?
   A. Frank was herding the cows to the corral.
   B. The cows needed some exercise.
   C. Frank was the winner in a horse race.

4.   There are two kinds of rocket fuel. The oldest kind is solid. It was first made long ago by people in China. They placed it in a tube in a rocket. Then they lit it. The fuel exploded. And the rocket went up into the air. The newer fuel is a liquid. It is used more often than the solid fuel. But it works the same way. It is put in a box at the bottom of the rocket. It explodes, and the rocket goes into the air.

_____   Which of these sentences is probably true?
   A. Rocket fuel has been used for a long time.
   B. A rocket costs much money to build.
   C. Rockets fly around the earth.

Name _____   Date _____

Read the story. Choose the sentence that best answers the question.

1. The bell rang. The boys came into the room. Some had their shirttails
sticking out of their pants. Each one had a bat or a ball. All had red faces. They
were glad to get into their seats. The teacher said it was time to get back to work.

_____ Which of these sentences is probably true?
  A. The boys had just come in from playing.
  B. The teacher yelled at the boys.
  C. The boys had just finished math.

2. Tony got up early each morning. He dressed, and then he helped his
mother cook breakfast. They cooked ham and eggs.
Tony set the table. His mother always gave him an
extra cinnamon bun for helping her.

_____ Which of these sentences is probably true?
  A. Tony loved to eat cinnamon buns.
  B. Tony was the last person to get out of bed.
  C. Tony helped his father.

3. Lisa tore the paper off the box. She could not wait to open it. There
was a wonderful brown duck inside. She placed it next to her other gifts.
She already had a book and a doll. Then she and her friends ran to the table.
Her dad brought in the cake.

_____ Which of these sentences is probably true?
  A. Lisa had a nice birthday party.
  B. Lisa didn't like to eat cake.
  C. Lisa's mother brought in the cake.

4. Bill had not seen Sam all week. He rode over to Sam's house.
He walked up and rang the doorbell. Sam's dad came to the
door. "Can Sam play?" asked Bill. Sam's father said, "No.
He is still in bed with a cold."

_____ Which of these sentences is probably true?
  A. Bill was not able to play.
  B. Bill wanted to play football.
  C. Sam had been sick for a few days.

COMPREHENSION: GRADE 3
ANSWER KEY

Unit I: Facts

Assessment, pp. 11-12
1. B
2. C
3. B
4. B
5. A
6. B
7. B
8. A

Lesson 1, pp. 13-14
1. A
2. C
3. C
4. C
5. A
6. C
7. B
8. A

Lesson 2, pp. 15-16
1. B
2. A
3. A
4. B
5. C
6. B
7. B
8. C

Lesson 3, pp. 17-18
1. C
2. C
3. C
4. B
5. A
6. C
7. B
8. A

Lesson 4, pp. 19-20
1. C
2. C
3. B
4. A
5. C
6. B
7. A
8. C

Lesson 5, pp. 21-22
1. C
2. B
3. B
4. A
5. C
6. B
7. C
8. B

Lesson 6, pp. 23-24
1. C
2. A
3. B
4. C
5. A
6. C
7. B
8. B

Unit II: Sequence

Assessment, pp. 25-26
1. 2, 1
2. A
3. C
4. B

Lesson 1, p. 28
1. 1, 2
2. C
3. A
4. B

Lesson 2, p. 30
1. 2, 1
2. A
3. C
4. C

Lesson 3, p. 32
1. 2, 1
2. A
3. C
4. B

Lesson 4, p. 34
1. 2, 1
2. C
3. C
4. B

Lesson 5, p. 36
1. 1, 2
2. C
3. A
4. B

Lesson 6, p. 38
1. 2, 1
2. A
3. B
4. C

Unit III: Context

Assessment, pp. 39-40
1. B
2. A
3. B
4. C
5. B
6. A
7. B
8. C

Lesson 1, p. 41
1. C
2. A
3. B
4. A

Lesson 2, p. 42
1. C
2. A
3. C
4. B

Lesson 3, p. 43
1. C
2. B
3. C
4. A

Lesson 4, p. 44
1. A
2. C
3. A
4. B

Lesson 5, p. 45
1. C
2. B
3. A
4. C

Lesson 6, p. 46
1. B
2. C
3. C
4. B

Lesson 7, p. 47
1. A
2. B
3. C
4. A

Lesson 8, p. 48
1. A
2. C
3. B
4. C

Lesson 9, p. 49
1. C
2. B
3. C
4. B

Lesson 10, p. 50
1. C
2. B
3. A
4. C

Lesson 11, p. 51
1. C
2. B
3. C
4. B

Lesson 12, p. 52
1. A
2. C
3. A
4. B

Unit IV: Main Idea

Assessment, pp. 53-54
1. A
2. A
3. C
4. B
5. A
6. C
7. B
8. B

Lesson 1, p. 55
1. A
2. B
3. A

Lesson 2, p. 56
1. B
2. A
3. A
4. C

Lesson 3, p. 57
1. B
2. A
3. B
4. C

Lesson 4, p. 58
1. B
2. C
3. C
4. A

Lesson 5, p. 59
1. B
2. A
3. B
4. C

Lesson 6, p. 60
1. A
2. B
3. C

Lesson 7, p. 61
1. C
2. A
3. B
4. B

Lesson 8, p. 62
1. B
2. A
3. C
4. C

Lesson 9, p. 63
1. B
2. B
3. C
4. A

Lesson 10, p. 64
1. B
2. B
3. C

Lesson 11, p. 65
1. A
2. A
3. B

Lesson 12, p. 66
1. B
2. A
3. A
4. B

Unit V: Conclusion
Assessment, pp. 67-68
1. C
2. A
3. A
4. A
5. B
6. C

Lesson 1, p. 69
1. A
2. B
3. B
4. C

Lesson 2, p. 70
1. A
2. B
3. C

Lesson 3, p. 71
1. A
2. C
3. C

Lesson 4, p. 72
1. B
2. B
3. C

Lesson 5, p. 73
1. A
2. C
3. A

Lesson 6, p. 74
1. C
2. B
3. C

Lesson 7, p. 75
1. B
2. C
3. B

Lesson 8, p. 76
1. A
2. C
3. B

Lesson 9, p. 77
1. C
2. A
3. B

Lesson 10, p. 78
1. A
2. B
3. C

Lesson 11, p. 79
1. B
2. A
3. C

Lesson 12, p. 80
1. C
2. B
3. A

Unit VI: Inference
Assessment, pp. 81-82
1. A
2. A
3. A
4. B
5. A
6. A
7. A
8. B

Lesson 1, p. 83
1. A
2. B
3. A

Lesson 2, p. 84
1. A
2. B
3. A

Lesson 3, p. 85
1. A
2. A
3. C
4. C

Lesson 4, p. 86
1. C
2. C
3. B

Lesson 5, p. 87
1. B
2. C
3. B

Lesson 6, p. 88
1. B
2. A
3. A
4. C

Lesson 7, p. 89
1. C
2. B
3. B
4. C

Lesson 8, p. 90
1. A
2. B
3. B

Lesson 9, p. 91
1. A
2. B
3. C
4. A

Lesson 10, p. 92
1. C
2. C
3. A
4. A

Lesson 11, p. 93
1. A
2. A
3. A
4. A

Lesson 12, p. 94
1. A
2. A
3. A
4. C